TEACHING
to Capture and Inspire
All Learners

Dedicated to Amari
Through your eyes, I see the world

STEPHEN G. PETERS

TEACHING
to Capture and Inspire
All Learners

Bringing
Your Best Stuff
Every Day!

Foreword by
Alan M. Blankstein

CORWIN PRESS
A SAGE Company
Thousand Oaks, CA 91320

For information:

Corwin Press
A SAGE Company
2455 Teller Road
Thousand Oaks,
  California 91320
www.corwinpress.com

SAGE Ltd.
1 Oliver's Yard
55 City Road
London EC1Y 1SP
United Kingdom

SAGE India Pvt. Ltd.
B 1/I 1 Mohan Cooperative
  Industrial Area
Mathura Road, New Delhi 110 044
India

SAGE Asia-Pacific Pte. Ltd.
33 Pekin Street #02-01
Far East Square
Singapore 048763

Printed in the United States of America.

Library of Congress Cataloging-in-Publication Data

Peters, Stephen G.
Teaching to capture and inspire all learners: bringing your best stuff every day!/Stephen G. Peters.
    p. cm.
Includes bibliographical references and index.
ISBN 978-1-4129-5873-8 (cloth)
ISBN 978-1-4129-5874-5 (pbk.)
   1. Effective teaching—United States. 2. Motivation in education—United States. 3. School improvement programs—United States. 4. Teacher-student relationships—United States. I. Title.

LB1025.3.P467 2008
371.102—dc22   2007033099

This book is printed on acid-free paper.

08   09   10   11   10   9   8   7   6   5   4   3   2

Acquisitions Editor:	Allyson P. Sharp
Editorial Assistant:	David Andrew Gray
Production Editor:	Cassandra Margaret Seibel
Copy Editor:	Barbara Ray
Typesetter:	C&M Digitals (P) Ltd.
Proofreader:	Doris Hus
Indexer:	Holly Day
Cover Designer:	Karine Hovsepian

Contents

Special List of Figures

Foreword

The passion that comes through when hearing Stephen Peters speak is echoed in this call to capture the students who are most often marginalized. Using an array of statistics and personal observations, Stephen calls on the heart and the conscience of the educator when asking you to "bring your best stuff every day" into the classroom. The most essential elements for success in *Teaching to Capture and Inspire All Learners: Bringing Your Best Stuff Every Day!* are the relationships formed between student and staff, and to this end, Stephen provides a continuous drumbeat of advice.

Unfettered by a prescriptive set of "how-to's," this book focuses more on the underlying values that drive behavior, as well as some of the "what does good teaching look like?" Many of these observations are drawn from Stephen's successes as a former school administrator. As such, this can serve as an excellent primer for discussion around the individual as well as collective values and commitments of the school staff. Addressing core questions such as "If all students can learn, why aren't they learning?" can engage staff for some time in important issues that all schools need to address to be their very best.

In addition, *Teaching to Capture and Inspire All Learners: Bringing Your Best Stuff Every Day!* provides numerous "to-do" or "to-consider" lists that may be considered in such a dialogue.

There are helpful tips for the new teacher who may be struggling with the real challenges of reaching today's students, and insights for veteran educators to consider in better understanding these same students. Overall, the "underdog" in our society is well represented and advocated for in this passionate plea for ALL students' success!

Alan M. Blankstein
September 2007

Preface

It is not the critic who counts: not the man who points out how the strong man stumbles or where the doer of deeds could have done better. The credit belongs to the man who is actually in the arena, whose face is marred by dust and sweat and blood, who strives valiantly, who errs and comes up short again and again, because there is no effort without error or shortcoming, but who knows the great enthusiasms, the great devotions; who spends himself for a worthy cause; who, at the best, knows, in the end, the triumph of high achievement, and who, at the worst, if he fails, at least he fails while daring greatly, so that his place shall never be with those cold and timid souls who knew neither victory nor defeat.

Teddy Roosevelt, April 23, 1910

Public education is facing its most critical times and one would find it difficult to argue with current statistical findings. However, in my travels, I have come face-to-face with teachers and leaders who actually are in the arena, whose faces are marred by dust and sweat and blood. I stand boldly with you as we continue to find answers to many of the complex questions facing us. I am confident that as we face some defeat, we will in the end know VICTORY for our students, ALL of them.

Teaching to Capture and Inspire All Learners evolved out of numerous experiences of being involved with schools that were first in categories one would want to be last in and last in categories one would want to be first in. Through a collaborative effort, effective teaming, and courageous leadership, we were able to transform these schools into national and state blue-ribbon schools in short periods of time.

Many years ago, researchers stressed the need for schools and school districts to understand that the change process takes on average three to five years to take shape. This book is written primarily to offer its readers a refreshing look into creating schools of passion and purpose filled with educators who finally realized our students don't have three to five years to wait for positive change. It has to happen now.

Chapters 1–3 lay the foundation for understanding the need for immediate change in our schools and the expanded roles of those responsible for cultivating this change process. Chapters 4–6 offer readers an in-depth look at the apparent reasons many of our students fall short of others sitting in the same classrooms of schools struggling to survive and meet the needs of this generation of learners. Chapters 7 and 8 introduce practical and specific strategies to principals, teachers, and schools that turn vision into operational strategies.

Throughout this book, each chapter opens with a main concept, statistic, or quote, and ends with a motivational summary. There are numerous reflection questions to assist in examining your own educational practices. By helping you carefully analyze your own philosophy about teaching, this resource will give you the opportunity to bring your best stuff every day.

This book offers hope to those in the field of education who may have lost hope and is dedicated to every student waiting to be captured, inspired, and taught in ways like never before. *Teaching to Capture and Inspire All Learners* will help even mediocre teachers become inspired to deliver quality at a higher level and will help leaders develop a deeper understanding of the importance of creating win-win experiences for ALL learners.

Acknowledgments

I thank God for another opportunity to capture and inspire educators, our true heroes. Thank you so much for everything you do for our students. A special thanks to my wife, Angela, and our children, Jillian, Jourdan, Xavier, and Maya, for allowing me to do what I do each day. Because of you, I am able to take my rightful place in this world. To Visionary Leaders Institute in Columbus, Ohio, The HOPE Foundation in Bloomington, Indiana, CaseNEX in Charlottesville, Virginia, and The Peters Group staff, may we continue to make much more than a difference in this world. To Dr. Ulysses Van Spiva, Dr. Robert Hahne, and the late Dr. J. Frank Sellew, thank you for everything you taught me about school leadership and life. To my dad, who continues to teach me through action, not words. How I wish the world were full of fathers like you. To Edward, welcome home.

Last, I wish to thank my editor, Allyson Sharp, and assistant editor, David Gray, for their wonderful ability to see beyond words, for turning my manuscript into a meaningful contribution to education.

This book is dedicated to my grandson, Amari Seldon. Through your eyes I clearly see that we can never quit or give up on the foundation of the most important gift in life—a quality education.

In loving memory of my mother, Charity Smalls Peters; brother, Lewis Clinton Peters; and father-in-law, Dr. William Waymer.

About the Author

 **Stephen G. Peters** has been a classroom teacher, assistant principal, principal, and director of secondary education. He has been in the field of education for more than 25 years, and most of his experiences have been in schools that made significant growth in short periods of time, thus resulting in both national and state blue ribbon distinction.

Peters has served on panels as an education expert with former U.S. Secretary of Education, Dr. Rod Paige, in Washington, D.C.

He is the author of three books and founder of The Gentlemen's Club, a program for at-risk and borderline males in public schools. Peters shares his practical strategies, philosophies, beliefs, and message of hope with organizations and school districts throughout the United States and Canada. He is CEO of The Peters Group, Inc., and also serves as a consultant with Visionary Leaders Institute and The HOPE Foundation.

He has been featured on television programs such as *America, America* and *The Oprah Winfrey Show.*

1

Appreciating Today's Students

We estimate that aggregate expenditures by 15- to 24-year-olds in the 15 urban areas with the highest concentration of multicultural youth will total $203 billion in 2007. This represents cumulative growth of 26.7%. (Montuori, 2003)

A 2004 study by the National Endowment for the Arts found that Hispanic and African-American males had the lowest rates of literary reading, at 18% and 30% respectively. Though reading rates were falling for all students, from 1992 to 2002 African Americans had the largest decline, from 45.6% to 37.1%. (Literary reading in dramatic decline, 2004)

I n order to help you bring your best stuff every day, this chapter will teach you how to do the following:

- Understand Today's Students and Today's Schools
- Understand the Power of Peer Influence
- Understand Media Influence
- Understand Families
- Have an Effective Team
- Appreciate Today's Students
- Have Belief and Hope

In today's data-happy era of accountability, testing, and No Child Left Behind, the most astonishing statistic in the whole field of education is the fact that, according to a *Time* article titled "Dropout Nation," 30% of America's high school students will leave high school without graduating. For Latinos and African Americans, the rate approaches an alarming 50%. Virtually no community, small or large, rural or urban, has escaped the problem (Thornburgh, 2006).

To make matters worse, at least a million illiterate students graduate from America's high schools each year. This means that these students cannot read, write, or use numbers sufficiently to get along in our society. According to the *Time* article, 13% of all American 17-year-olds are functionally illiterate; among minority students, the rate climbs to 40%. The U.S. Department of Education estimates that our educational system has already left us with 24 million functional illiterates. These are not students who never went to school; these are students who, for the most part, have spent 8–12 years in our public schools (Thornburgh, 2006).

We are beyond the crisis point and must act quickly to combat the mediocrity that exists in our classrooms. But, in order for us to act, we must realize that we've been acted on by the ills of society. The damage done to our children by the breakdown of the American family is at the very core of our dilemma (The Center for Reclaiming America, 1997). Before we can begin to go forward, we must look back over time and identify the core elements and beliefs that have mysteriously vanished, leaving the foundation of our students' security broken.

When I became a principal in the early 1990s, my staff and I began looking at our competition. We learned that we were not competing with other schools in our district or in other districts, but with the "home invasion" of our society and students as a whole. From our research, we identified five sources that strongly influence children (in decreasing order of negative influence):

- Television/Media
- Peers
- Church
- School
- Home

We then developed a plan to combat or offset the power of the negative influences by moving from understanding the problems to creating solutions for all learners in our school. For many of us involved, it came down to remembering the major influences in our lives as children and how there was always a choice to be made. Unfortunately, many students today are making negative choices and receiving negative consequences as a result.

From the list above, in what order did the major influences in your childhood fall? What other influences shaped your childhood?

Understanding our past is important because it allows us to understand the changes that have occurred, as well as their impact on society and our schools.

UNDERSTAND TODAY'S STUDENTS AND TODAY'S SCHOOLS

Office referrals in schools are increasing each year. In large part, students are angry at the adults in their lives who continue to disappoint them. This anger grows at school every day that someone says or does something to irritate them further. When students hold feelings in long enough, those feelings usually don't manifest in a manner we'd like. The first person to confront today's students will in turn be confronted. Therefore, it is important for us to create win-win situations with our students. The more win-win situations we're able to create, the more deposits we make into that relationship with our students. We all know what happens when we make deposits. There may also be times when we need to make a withdrawal. Understanding what students are going through will give us opportunities to deliver better quality education to each one of our students.

Today's School

Today, we talk about "vision," which is the order of business in schools. Unfortunately, in some schools, that vision is blurred. While participating in research, many students and teachers expressed their desire for better school conditions (Peters, 2006). The common theme was they both desired a safe and secure environment, caring adults or students, and an opportunity to teach or learn. When we look at this, the answer seems simple, doesn't it? If the teachers and students want the same thing, then why is it so hard to produce in our schools? However, I am a firm believer that not enough students and, yes, teachers desire the same thing.

Schools tend to have elaborately written vision and mission statements hanging on their walls; they are so well written and sound so good, but the alarming fact is that teachers, students, staff, and parents are unaware of their significance. We should all adopt the same mission: No Child Left Out!

There is so much we can learn from small learning communities (which, by the way, existed long ago), courageous leadership, differentiated instructional approaches, curriculum mapping, and effective school cultures, but we must first develop great relationships with our students and other educators within our school because good is no longer good enough to produce schools of quality.

UNDERSTAND THE POWER OF PEER INFLUENCE

Peer groups provide one of the strongest influences available to our students today and continue to gain power in a society that appears to pay more attention to money and fame than to whether a child can read and write.

The nation's attention has long been captured by the plight of increasing numbers of students in circumstances that place them at risk of educational failure, particularly in inner-city communities. People in these communities face poverty, lack of employment opportunities, poor health care, and crime, all of which jeopardize quality of life.

In years past, older siblings, friends of the family, church members, responsible teens, and programs such as the YMCA provided an extension of the family's core support system. Younger brothers and sisters looked up to their older siblings and parents had high expectations for their children despite the shortage of money or material possessions. Parents who lacked a formal education wanted more for their children. In the worst case scenario, young people who made bad decisions would reflect and try harder to make the right one the next time they were faced with a similar situation. Today, rap stars, negative peer influence, promiscuous teens, and gangs team up with television and media influences to make an indelible imprint into the hearts, minds, and spirits of today's students (Powell, 2007). In some school communities, gang members have replaced brothers and sisters as role models, providing consistent patterns of behavior that provide a false sense of trust and family. Today, a bad choice can end in death, with no second chances.

Although some households continue to struggle to put food on the table and clothes on the backs of young children in the home, the American retail economy experienced a 17.4% increase in sales in 2003, which can be traced directly to the spending of urban and inner-city youth as they accumulate new sneakers, jewelry, stylish clothing, and other material possessions they define as "necessities" (Montuori, 2003).

Students today struggle to develop and maintain an identity separate from the identity their peers create for them. According to many of the students, the pressure is unbelievable at times. Contrary to the picture painted by the media, this issue does not only affect poor, urban students—middle- and upper-class students are affected as well. One U.S. school district with a median household income of approximately $300,000 a year also has one of the highest rates of suicide among its students entering high school.

Understand Media Influence

Every student entering a school today is influenced greatly by television and other media outlets like never before in history. On average, our students are watching television and DVDs, playing video games, listening to iPods, text messaging, surfing the Internet, or being influenced by other associated outlets 30 hours or more a week (Davison, Francis, & Birch, 2005). Imagine the impact of doing anything 30 plus hours a week! It is difficult to separate and rank these major influences in terms of which has the most damaging impact on our students' lives. More important, there is an increasing need for us to understand the collective power of these influences. In the past, families watched television programs together to gain knowledge and understanding or to be entertained through wholesome content. The programs were appropriate for children and often provided insight into a subject for later discussion by viewers. There were also a limited number of channels for public viewing pleasure.

Today, however, many households receive countless television programs that offer a wide array of content. And aside from television, Web surfing, chat rooms, and blogs are popular with today's youth. Although some of the content on the Internet is not appropriate for our students, they are viewing it at an alarming rate. The negative impact of this media consumption could be underrated because the jury is still out on the number of students making decisions based on what they saw or heard on television or a computer. The influence is steady, consistent, and powerful. The images can be more harmful to students who are too young to understand them. The fantasy of television and technology becomes the reality of many of our students.

As schools, we have very little control over the amount of time our students watch television or the content of what they watch, but we do have a great influence over what they experience when they are with us. Over time, I have become convinced that we spend enough time with them to make a significant impact on their lives; we can help them become human beings who seek knowledge and understanding of how the world really works and how they can play a key role in making it a better place.

Education is the only way we will ever be free.

Understand Families

The home environment should be the most influential of all to our students. It provides an abundance of resources even in families of limited economic means or those facing hardships such as divorce, death, or chronic illness. Parents serve as children's first teachers and should provide knowledge about the world as well as functional connections to the larger community. However, what is expected is not always provided.

A positive family life is incredibly important for children's well-being.

> ❧ ❧
>
> **What are other influences that have affected today's students?**

Short-term prospective studies demonstrate that many family-related factors protect against adversity, including a positive parent-child relationship, family cohesion, warmth, assigned chores, responsibilities for the family's well-being, an absence of discord, and other secure childhood attachments. Other family attributes associated with school success include emphasis on good attendance, high expectations, consistent practices, assistance with homework, and reading to children daily. But many of our students do not have this family foundation in place, and many are also attempting to provide these elements to their younger siblings as well as extended family members.

Many students are resilient and determined in many respects to make it in the world; they show an amazing ability to keep going regardless of all that's happening around them. And we in the schools can help. Even without strong families, there is always hope for our students and schools as long as there are knowledgeable, caring adults rallying around them and believing in them. To produce award-winning schools, it is important that educators believe in educating students regardless of their family backgrounds, how they look, or where they are from. We must believe in unconditional positive regard: failure is not an option for any student. The blueprint for our success may differ from that of others, but it will always center on the most important question educators can ask: "Is it in the best interest of the students?"

Have an Effective Team

While serving as principal of my first school, which had 1,200 students, I realized the power of peer influence. We found in most instances that 90% of our problems were being caused by 10% of our student population. Understanding this was one of the most important elements in our attempt to turn around a school on a collision course with disaster. We had 135 adults who cared about our students, but they lacked the authority to engage them in a relevant manner.

I will never forget the morning of October 11, 1996, as I stood in the auditorium of our school awaiting the arrival of 30 of our most hardcore students to arrive for a meeting I called. Nothing could have prepared me for what was about to take place as I began requesting help from the very students who were causing the majority of the problems in and around our school. Their first reaction was to ask whether they were going to be suspended again, and I responded that I couldn't suspend them because I needed their help. After recovering from the shock, most of them began to listen to my plan. These students would become part of my management team to assist me in the running of the school. There were certain requirements such as appropriate dress and behavior, but there were also rewards and incentives for them such as eating at restaurants, attending professional sporting events, and other activities. The hardest group in our school to reach was beginning to come around, and I was hopeful for a moment.

This all changed as I laid out the dress requirement for members of my management team: They all had to wear white shirts and ties. The reaction was as I expected. Several of the students, who, incidentally, were all boys, began shifting in their seats as if to say, "you must be out of your mind." We were eventually able to convince this group of highly disengaged male students that this was best for them and us. Many of these young men came from the troubled Winona Middle School. Unless something intervened to offer them a chance at something better, these young men's past lives would have determined their futures. The group I formed that day, which became known as "The Gentlemen's Club," offered them a chance. On the day of their unveiling, newspaper photographers and reporters were there to greet, interview, and encourage them; the resulting front-page article was titled, "Principal Turns Problems into Princes." There was a buzz around school about this group of students who were making an attempt to collaborate with their school community to make a positive difference.

The Gentlemen's Club

Our school was first in areas you wish to be last in and last in areas you wish to be first in. The school day was characterized by violence, lack of attendance, repeat offenders, and disrespectful students and adults. As principal, I knew we had to find an intervention strategy that worked. After that initial meeting that led to the formation of the Gentlemen's Club, our students, teachers, administrators, and community leaders banded together to make sure our school grounds were safe and that something positive was taking place in each classroom every day. The image of our school began to improve slowly. In fact, after two years the school was in pretty good shape, but we were still not reaching our targeted male students. We could always suspend them, but that would not solve the problem—it would merely change its location from the school to the streets.

We developed the Gentlemen's Club (GC) to serve as a lifeline to save countless young men from falling through the cracks. The GC would show the students that there was another way to live their lives. It would prove to them that one need not let the rhythm of the streets dictate the tune they will sing in their lives.

Collaboratively, we decided these young men needed a new direction, one that would enlighten them, expose them to a world outside of their own, and ultimately restore hope to their young lives. They needed real mentors, adults who could give them reasons to dream again. Through teacher and staff recommendations, we compiled a list of young men in need of such intervention. The list of nominees included students ranging from class cutters and smokers to gang members and felons. Their disciplinary records (many longer than the wingspan of an NBA player) included offenses for attendance, disrespect, insubordination, harassment, hitting, profanity, disruption, fighting, and assault. Eventually, we narrowed the list to 30 young men who probably would have appeared in every teacher's rogues' gallery. The team of faculty and staff members who volunteered to work with the Gentlemen's Club had their work cut out for them. Fortunately, more help than they ever imagined was headed their way.

In college, most of us had read the now-classic *Dress for Success*, and we knew appearance greatly influenced people's impressions, especially first impressions. But, although a crisp white shirt and a tie can make a remarkable change in one's appearance and the perception of others, you can't wear them if you don't have them. Most of our young men lacked a white shirt, a tie, or the financial resources to acquire them.

Through the efforts of our teachers and school community, the principal's office was soon filled with shirts, ties, and sport coats—every size, shape, and color imaginable. For a while, it seemed we were transforming our offices and conference rooms into men's clothing outlets. After we had the white shirts and ties, and after considerable effort and an equal amount of spray starch, our fine and practical arts teacher transformed them into "crisp" white shirts. She also developed a handbook of etiquette and conducted "manners workshops" with our club members. Our rallying cry became "there is never an excuse for bad manners."

Our faculty advisor/GC facilitator explained the fine points of knotting a tie. Thanks to the efforts of our school family, on Mondays our 30 select young men would be wearing white shirts and ties to school. Instead of being suspended over and over again, these young men were fast becoming part of our school's management team, using their influence in a positive way.

The key component of the Gentlemen's Club is collaboration. We employed the concept of reciprocal respect in all of our dealings with each other and encouraged our school community to do the same. We began to see immediate results from the teamwork and continued to grow together to understand the term *synergy*. The most powerful lesson for many of the adults in our building was to understand the influence these 30 young male students exerted over their peers. The immediate positive results included better attendance, fewer behavioral problems, and higher academic achievement. More important, we were onto something big in terms of cultivating a more positive school environment that would produce positive results for our students.

APPRECIATE TODAY'S STUDENTS

When teachers and principals exhibit high expectations and concern and serve as appropriate role models, they help militate against the likelihood of academic failure, particularly for students in difficult life circumstances. In order for educators to build productive relationships and connections with students, it is important to understand what is going on in students' lives away from school. Close relationships with educators can reduce students' stress and provide positive support throughout difficult times. Educators can not only provide instructional support for academic content and skills, but also serve as confidants and internal support for students. Effective educators help their students develop values and attitudes needed to persevere and excel in their schoolwork. They introduce new and meaningful experiences that make learning interesting and relevant to today's students. The most important thing educators can do is to promote educational resilience by encouraging students to master new experiences, believe in their own efficacy, and take responsibility for their own learning.

We know now that all students, including those with special needs, can surpass high academic standards when provided with relevant and stimulating content and instruction, as well as support, tailored to their individual strengths and learning needs. By contrast, information and subject matter that are disconnected from students' experiences, culture, and needs contribute to their learning problems and ultimately their failure to connect and lack of desire to do so.

However, it is important to remember that the school, the family, or the community acting alone cannot address the multiple risks and adversities that today's generation of students faces. Rather, the resources within these three contexts must be harnessed if educators are to solve the educational, psychological, and social issues that confront families and our students.

The students enrolled in our schools are bright, resilient, eager, and curious, and all have the ability and desire to learn; the problem is reaching out to them in ways that engage them. Researchers using an action research design conducted a series of intervention studies on how schools can be more responsive to today's students by changing their organization and using innovative approaches to service delivery. These studies focused on the areas of (1) implementing small unit organization to improve student engagement, (2) collegiality among staff, and (3) cross-disciplinary collaboration (Oxley, 1994). Findings suggest the importance of the following:

- Changing the mind-set of administrators and the teaching staff on how learning takes place.
- Implementation of coordinated approaches to organizing school resources.
- Staff development that focuses on developing strategies and expertise for meeting the diverse needs of students.

In several schools studied, these changes were found to produce significant improvements in teachers' attitudes toward school and ability to institute radical changes in the service of students, as well as enhanced student motivation and improved student achievement (Nash, n.d.).

Schools are finding themselves in a precarious position, serving both as a delivery system to their students and as the foundation for the delivery to take place. To deliver quality to our students and school community, we must understand that quality is never an accident. It is the result of good intentions and skillful execution; it represents the wisest choice from many alternatives.

Schools truly have more opportunities to become successful when the adults in the school understand the power and authority they have to restore hope to students. Those opportunities are increased each time a teacher recognizes another chance to capture and inspire a student (discussed further in Chapter 7). Students understand and appreciate adults who exhibit caring attitudes toward them and tend to work harder for these adults. In the end, it will not be those who have the most content knowledge whose students soar, it will be those who have content knowledge and the ability to capture and inspire ALL learners.

HAVE BELIEF AND HOPE

There is an element to improving schools and students' academic performance that transcends any method or approach:

the attitude and spirit of the team. We have to understand that we will never stop learning about ourselves, our students, each other, or the world as a whole. When we embrace the reality of becoming continuous and lifelong learners, there is some humility attached. There is a strong measure of independence in our profession, and it is often difficult to come to terms with the fact that there may be a better way to teach something than the way we have always done it.

Unless:

1. There is a belief that regardless of a school's social or economic circumstances, improvement can occur.

2. "I" becomes "we" and we work collaboratively to accomplish all of our goals, remembering that we are here for our students and keeping their best interests in our minds and hearts.

3. We arrive each morning having confidence in our collective ability, knowing that even if we fall short, there are others teaching beyond their capacity today.

4. Leaders understand the need to consistently validate and affirm teachers and support staff.

5. We constantly remind ourselves that students are our #1 priority.

To help us generate and maintain hope, we must celebrate and elevate success. We should study other schools and systems that have overcome great odds, taking learning about their successes as well as their stumbling blocks. But to be most effective, we must resist the impulse to leap prematurely to solutions before understanding the nature of the problem. Before selecting and elaborating on a potential solution, we should always carefully consider its consistency with what we know from research and our sense of its potential impact on student learning.

As we embark on this remarkable journey, we must never lose sight of the fact that we are in the midst of a hostile takeover—a takeover by certain aspects of society of our students' hearts, minds, and spirits. We must elevate our teaching and communication skills to a level that will lessen the power of the grip that certain harmful parts of the world have on our students. **We must bring our best stuff every day!**

Think of a success you had with a student. Think of a failure you had with a student. How did the situations compare and how were they different?

CHAPTER SUMMARY

In years past, the majority of students entered school buildings ready to learn. A loving, caring family created a foundation of consistent practices and expectations that bolstered this state of readiness. Many of today's students lack the foundation many of us had while growing up, and as a result, are influenced heavily by each other as well as today's ever-changing society that values the material aspects of the world far more than education. However, through strong collaboration and positive belief systems, such as the formation of the Gentlemen's Club to transform troublemaking students into leaders, many schools and teachers are helping students succeed by understanding the root of what divides us from them.

Chapter 2 discusses the important role and the characteristics of school leaders. Families and students are different, and so is the role of leaders, which has expanded to the degree that many are calling for increased preparation and training for teachers and administrative staff. Through the development of effective teams who understand and appreciate today's students and families, school leaders are beginning to embrace the changing nature of school leadership.

2

The Expanded Role of School Leaders

Quality is never an accident. It is the result of good intentions and skillful execution; it represents the wisest choice from many alternatives.

During the past decade, numerous states, localities, and foundations have launched initiatives to recruit and train better principals. What these efforts share is a recognition that school leaders exert a powerful influence on teacher quality and student learning. (Mazzeo, 2003)

By the end of this chapter, in order to bring your best stuff every day, you should understand:

- Principal Leadership Styles
- The Changing Nature of School Leadership
- How to Create "Win-Win" With Teachers
- Leadership Versus Management
- Characteristics of School Building Leadership

According to researchers Philip Hallinger and Ronald Heck, school principals "exercise a measurable, though indirect, effect on school effectiveness and student achievement." Leadership appears to particularly affect the quality of teaching in schools (Schiff, 2002).

School leaders provide focus and direction to curriculum and teaching and manage the organization efficiently to support student and adult learning. Principals also evaluate teachers and make decisions about classroom assignments and delivery of instruction. When classroom instruction is weak in underperforming schools, significant responsibility rests with the principal.

The evidence suggests that quality school leaders understand teaching, and their staff respects them. They are willing to hold themselves and others responsible for student learning and to help teachers become better at making this happen. As noted researcher Richard Elmore (2000) puts it:

> The job of administrative leaders is primarily about enhancing the skills and knowledge of the people in the organization, creating a common culture of expectations around the use of those skills and knowledge, holding the various pieces of the organization together in a productive relationship with each other, and holding individuals accountable for their contributions to the collective results. (p. 16)

How each school leader performs these tasks will inevitably vary. Principals have different leadership styles and will ultimately do what becomes comfortable to them, but research suggests three primary modes of leading that promote student learning: principal as entrepreneur, principal as organizer, and principal as instructional leader.

Principal Leadership Styles

Principal as Entrepreneur

Effective school leaders develop and sustain a focus on instructional improvement and student learning while protecting teachers from the intrusions from the outside environment (Sebring & Bryk, 2000).

Principal as Organizer

Effective principals bring to their schools innovative individuals and innovative ideas, programs, and instructional strategies that can improve teaching while maintaining a coherent reform agenda. They also engage teachers, parents and families, and community members as collaborators and leaders in school improvement efforts (Newmann, 2001).

Principal as Instructional Leader

Effective school leaders build data-driven professional communities that hold all individuals accountable for student learning and instructional improvement. They do this by managing time and financial resources to build teachers' professional skills and knowledge (Louis & Kruse, 1995).

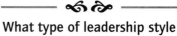

What type of leadership style do you most demonstrate?

Research suggests that many current and potential school leaders lack the skills necessary to lead in today's schools. A 2001 Public Agenda report found that 29% of superintendents believe the quality of principals has declined measurably in recent years (Farkas, Johnson, Duffet, & Foleno, 2001). There are several possible reasons for this drop-off:

Principals are being forced into the role of managers because of the increasing demands of today's students.

Principals cannot gain experience as instructional leaders because disciplining students has become the top priority in most places.

Principal positions are no longer attractive to quality candidates because of the increasing demands of today's schools.

Solutions to address these concerns include the following:

School districts must begin sharing their success stories with the world. There are wonderful things happening in many of our schools, but only those closely associated with the school are even aware of those positive stories. This may attract a broader pool of leadership candidates.

Superintendents must aggressively recruit and retain quality school leader candidates.

School districts should develop leaders from within their very own system through various means, such as leadership mentoring and leadership training programs that lead to assistant principal and principal positions.

Superintendents should collaborate with higher education agencies to promote and attract leadership candidates coming out of their certification programs.

Superintendents should form alliances with county governments to offer leadership training to select individuals along with members of other city and county employees, thus providing a wide range of training.

THE CHANGING NATURE OF SCHOOL LEADERSHIP

One likely source of administrative dissatisfaction is the changing nature of school leadership. Historically, school leaders were expected to perform managerial and political roles. Today's schools require a new kind of principal, according to the Institute for Educational Leadership, one whose main responsibility will be defined in terms of instructional leadership focusing on strengthening teaching and learning.

An important aspect of strengthening teaching is recognition, which both business and industry tell us may be the most important and effective aspect of leadership (Grissmer & Kirby, 1997). In order for teachers to work effectively together, their accomplishments must be both recognized and celebrated. Sincere, consistent praise may be the most overlooked ingredient in results-oriented leadership.

When I was a teacher, it always made a difference to me to receive informal notes from the principal. It helped me feel validated and affirmed as one of the team members making great things happen for students every day. When I became a principal, I began using my Sunday evenings to write notes to my teachers and staff members thanking them for specific things. General letters work, but people tend to be more appreciative when it is clear why you are taking the time to do this. Figure 2.1 shows an example of one of the Sunday evening notes.

Figure 2.1   A Sunday Evening Letter

Dear Mrs. Brown,

I saw you handle a student conflict in the hallway last Friday that could have resulted in a student or students being harmed. You did an excellent job removing them from the hallway and prevented this incident from exploding. This school is a better place because of teachers like you.

Thank you so much for what you do every day!

Sincerely,

Your principal, Stephen

These letters became part of our new culture and made teachers and staff members feel special, but, most important, appreciated and validated. I didn't have to spend any money to do this, and it was not a mandate from anyone—just common sense that went a long way to secure buy-in from our hard-working teachers and staff. These simple notes went a long way toward our efforts to transform our school into a place of passion and purpose.

Schools today lack the "spark" of schools in past decades. The energy was different then because students came to school ready to learn and understood their sole purpose for being there. Parents reinforced what the school enforced, resulting in a win-win situation. School leaders today must create as many win-win situations as possible as they strive to create schools of excellence.

CREATING WIN-WIN WITH TEACHERS

Many people argue that new principals have little to offer until they have worked long enough to gain the valuable experience necessary to begin making informed decisions. I had the very opposite experience as a new, inexperienced principal and would like to offer hope to those of you who may not have spent long enough in the system to be accepted as a "quality" leader. By some people's

—— ❧ ❦ ——
What can you do immediately in your school to create a win-win situation?

standards, quantity matters, but by the standards of our students and those who love them, *quality* matters most.

With this in mind, our administrative team set out in our first year to change the culture—the very foundation—of our school. What we discovered as we laid this new foundation was interesting and exciting.

We all had issues. Our underlying belief systems were not aligned with our surface belief systems. Chapter 4 discusses this in more detail.

We had to take a personal inventory and begin to realize that those issues that we exposed could ultimately destroy our efforts. We were headed in the right direction, but we needed strong and courageous leadership. We wanted our teachers to believe when they arrived each morning that this was the best place for them to work. We created a climate of trust and belief in each other through various experiences and knew we had something special happening, but there was still something missing. Eventually, we all discovered there was a difference between leadership and management. This new understanding required us to change our daily operational strategies so we could become instructional leaders while still managing our school functions. We learned several things about leading and managing.

Things to Remember

• It's important to try to involve teachers in the decision-making process. Ask for input and opinions in faculty meetings, department meetings, and school leadership team meetings. Use a faculty suggestion box to encourage contributions from those who are reluctant to share openly. When teachers are involved in the decision-making process, they tend to work harder to successfully implement programs.

• Create a climate of trust as you work through issues with each other, as well as with students and parents. School leaders should always communicate with clarity and honesty. Regardless of how tough issues become, clarity and honesty are always appreciated. You must earn trust, which in turn will serve as a vehicle for many positive experiences.

• Operate from the position of reciprocal respect. Today's students and staff appreciate being respected. If you need a student to remove his hat, instead of saying, "take your hat off," you should say, "would you mind removing your hat, please?" This measure of reciprocal respect leaves the student with dignity.

• Identify teacher-leaders and create opportunities for them to function in this capacity. It is usually easy to identify leaders, who tend to operate as leaders daily. Spend time cultivating relationships with potential leaders. Assign them to committees and teams that function beyond their classroom role, such as deans of students or administrative assistants.

• Make yourself available as often as possible to your teachers as access is often considered opportunity when it comes to creating win-win scenarios. The principal's office should be empty during the school day; as a school leader, the principal should be out assisting with the overall operation of the school and interacting with staff, such as during cafeteria duty, hall duty, and bus duty. Those wishing to increase opportunity and availability should institute an open door office policy.

LEADERSHIP VERSUS MANAGEMENT

The core elements of school leadership rest with the expectations of those evaluating our principals, who expect such things as a safe and orderly environment, higher test scores, better attendance, lower dropout rates, and more students in advanced placement classes. Many of our school leaders are confused by the constant demands placed on them and on their teachers and support staff. The confusion is a result of the equal importance placed on leadership and management; both are equally important, but they must be separated in order to understand the function of each one in an effective school setting.

As a new assistant principal, I found myself surrounded by experienced leaders who seemed to function each day with amazing grace and courage. I began to absorb as much knowledge as possible while working with them. I discovered that strong and courageous leadership is the foundation for any school or system's success. In this school, the standard system of operation was built on lateral management—everyone at every level was empowered to be a leader with respect to their specific delivery of services. It was an amazing experience for me, one that shaped my future as a school leader and central office administrator.

Schools improve when educators' passion, purpose, and effort unite and each person accepts the school's mission. It is important for leaders to recognize the vital function of their job, which is to provide a safe and secure environment that fosters high student achievement. The kind of significant improvement needed in schools will not occur in isolation. In order for improvement to be sustained over time, each member of the team of educators must understand that on a day when one member struggles, there are others operating beyond their capacity.

The current school system was designed in the 1950s, and we continue to attempt to fine-tune something that has exceeded its own capacity. During a recent conversation, six new principals shared their frustration about the difficulty of meeting the high expectations placed on them and the consistent lack of resources and tools provided to meet them. The good news is that these young leaders possess the talent, desire, resilience, and commitment to all of our children—not to mention their belief that failure of any kind for any student is simply never an option.

One of the most effective means to breed success in schools is to emphasize a goal-oriented culture, thus eliminating competing agendas and other distractions that make it difficult to maintain focus. School leaders who are successful at creating these cultures have the following characteristics.

CHARACTERISTICS OF SCHOOL-BUILDING LEADERSHIP

Strong and effective instructional leadership

- Directing school staff time and energy to instructional issues
- Developing a collective sense of responsibility for school improvement among staff
- Securing resources and effective training for teachers
- Providing opportunities for teachers to collaborate on instructional improvement
- Creating additional time for active instruction
- Helping staff persist in the face of adversity

Clear school mission

- Student learning is defined as a top priority
- School staff have a sense of community and collective responsibility for school improvement
- The mission is clearly developed so that everyone can understand and apply it

(Continued)

(Continued)

Continuous staff development for
teachers and support staff

- Teachers and staff learn together within a building and collaborate to improve student learning
- Professional development opportunities are aligned with specific goals

Communication and collaboration
among teachers and staff

- Teachers work together within and across grade levels to align instruction to state standards and assessments and to create program consistency
- Classroom teachers and specialists collaborate on instruction
- Peers coach each other
- Teachers and staff work together with one mission: to help students

---

Seeing these crucial skills in operation daily has helped me recognize them in teachers. It is imperative to identify potential leaders in a school and develop and support them in such a way as to allow them to rise to their potential. Because it requires incredible effort to transform a school in a manner that can be sustained over time, everyone needs to be on board and operate in varied roles to make it happen.

What characteristics are you strong in and which one could you improve on?

In order for schools to understand the dynamics of their expanded role, they must interpret the language being sent by our critics. The main reason society is so critical of educators is our inability to increase student learning. As principals we must find ways to make learning exciting and relevant for our students, and the best way to do that is to start with those who deliver the instruction. The focal point of any school is its leader. Leaders in schools who engage all learners and increase student achievement share the following skills:

1. They model learning, i.e., they exhibit the behavior they want teachers to display.

Effective leaders may attend professional development training sessions to keep abreast of best practices or simply to sharpen their skills. They may also take an active role in faculty-staff book study groups as a member of the school's team. Leaders model behavior by allowing others to see them actively doing what they talk about. When teachers attend content-area in-services or workshops and see their principal there learning alongside them, it is a powerful demonstration of that principal's commitment to the school.

2. They are belief-driven and provide specific reasons for others to learn by encouraging high expectations of teachers, students, and staff

Nobody rises to low expectations, so leaders must set high expectations when communicating the overall vision and mission of the school. These expectations should be purpose-driven, and both specific and general roles should be defined so that each teacher or staff member realizes the power of a synergistic approach to delivering quality to ALL learners.

3. They encourage continuous growth in a supportive learning environment

To encourage growth among teachers and staff members, it is important to make opportunities available. Those opportunities may come from outside the school, but effective leaders will still open doors through a supportive environment.

4. They lead by example and make expectations clear

Leaders who are making a positive difference have the desire and ability to perform the same kinds of tasks they ask others to do. They embrace opportunities to serve as facilitators instead of bosses, and while doing so they effectively communicate both general and specific target goals.

5. They always provide the resources needed for excellence

Because they are essentially the CEOs of their schools, leaders must determine the needs of those who are actively engaged in the daily grind of producing results, and they must also hold those people accountable for target results. In order to do this, leaders must provide the tools those in the trenches need to perform their duties. This is a #1 priority.

Truly effective leadership should not rest on the shoulders of one individual, however; it should be a cooperative effort involving a number of individuals from every level in the hierarchy, with a direct focus on helping the students in the classrooms.

A study released recently by the Center for Reinventing Public Education at the University of Washington found that the new school leader need not be the standard-bearer in all areas of leadership. Commissioned by the Wallace Foundation, the study included interviews with 150 educators, including principals, vice-principals, and teachers, in 21 public, private, elementary, secondary, traditional, and charter schools. The final report stated that schools now need leadership in seven critical areas (Portin, Schneider, DeArmond, & Gundlach, 2003).

SEVEN CRITICAL AREAS OF SCHOOL LEADERSHIP

1. Instruction

Consistent observation and timely feedback are essential if teachers are to provide stimulating and relevant instruction. Therefore, effective leaders must have general content knowledge of what they are observing. Further, they must team with others who have more specific instructional knowledge, thus forming a knowledgeable and supportive network for quality instructional delivery.

2. Culture

Understanding and embracing the diverse cultures in our society is one of the most critical needs in our schools. Leaders must emphasize that all cultures should be respected, embraced, and celebrated, and they must make sure that this value transcends all the barriers that may present themselves.

3. Managerial Duties

Principals must attend to managerial duties and responsibilities if they are to lead today's schools. More effective leaders tend to delegate the majority of these responsibilities to able assistants.

4. Human Resources

A background in human resources helps principals improve their chances of leading an effective school. The more quality teachers and staff members you can place in front of today's students, the more opportunities your school is going to have to provide learners with a world-class education.

(Continued)

(Continued)

5. Strategic Planning

The strategic planning process has always been and continues to be an important vehicle for orchestrating a vision and making it a reality. Leaders must have experience in planning for and with others to ensure that goals are realistic and attainable. They must also have the ability to assess at the appropriate times and intervals to attain benchmarks for success.

6. External Development

Leaders are finding external sources of support beneficial, such as inviting community members, businesses, and adults in the general school area to extend services to their students and school community. An example of this would be a school agreeing to host a Rotary Club or Kiwanis Club.

7. Micropolitical

Once reserved for superintendents, school leadership is fast becoming a political position. Presently, school boards and districts are training potential candidates well in advance of their appointments to understand the parameters of politics and its impact on schools and school systems. The Chamber of Commerce is the central source of programs around the country that supply this specific training for future school leaders.

I admit that I was a horrible manager, but I felt quite differently about my leadership qualities. Knowing my limitations, I set out to surround myself with great managers, which gave me the opportunity to truly lead instead of being saddled with day-to-day managerial duties. My vice-principal was responsible for those day-to-day responsibilities, and she made up for what she might have lacked in experience with natural, instinctive leadership qualities. Her strength was managerial, whereas mine was leadership and communication.

By dividing the responsibilities this way, we had created a win-win situation for our school and students.

If a school is fortunate enough to find an inspiring and innovative leader who is able to make positive change happen, then a key question is what happens if the principal leaves? In our case, after I left the school to become a central office administrator, the vice-principal became the principal and did not miss a beat. I recommended her for the job and she eventually received it despite some reluctance from certain people who believe that you have to have lots of experience to be an effective leader. It comes down to the age-old question of how to gain experience if not given the opportunity? Two years after her appointment, school-level indicators were soaring in every area assessed and she was named "principal of the year" in our state.

Make a list of your strengths and weaknesses as a school leader. What steps can you make to improve in your weak areas?

As you continue to process and internalize the pages of this book, we encourage you to become a courageous leader and know that change in our schools has to occur now. Our students cannot wait three to five years for substantive change to take place. They depend on us to provide schools of passion and purpose where failure is never an option. To improve our schools, we must continue to innovate as leaders and adopt the attitude that we are providing safe, secure, and stimulating environments for our next generation. We should be teaching them as if they were our own biological children. Our students deserve no less. What a measurement to lead by!

CHAPTER SUMMARY

The role of school leaders has expanded to such a degree that they must understand its changing nature, obtain the necessary skills to adapt to these changes, and all the while maintain the focus on helping our students learn. Successful leaders can help create a culture that has at its core high expectations for everyone, coupled with the belief that all students are capable of achieving success. The expanded role of leaders challenges them to assemble high-performance teams to cope with demands that would be impossible for one person to handle.

Chapter 3 introduces the new realities of teaching, along with successful delivery systems designed to promote learning in a stimulating and relevant environment.

3

The Expanded Role of Teachers

Our greatest accomplishment is to be sure there is a teacher in every classroom, every day, who makes every student feel like a human being.

In this chapter, in order to bring your best stuff every day, you should understand the following:

- The Realities of Teaching
- Successful Delivery Systems
- Teacher Personality Types
- How to Avoid Blind Spots
- Knowledge Work

Many years ago, one of my former teachers called me up to her desk. It was the last day of school and she wanted me to know I was ready to move on to the next grade. She proceeded to do the same with all of my classmates, one by one. When we had all gone before her, she asked all of us to stand and asked us a question. The question was, "why are you so ready?" The answer to that question was, "because you taught us."

She operated under a belief system that teachers who believe they *can* make a difference *do* make a difference.

There are many dedicated, hard-working teachers in our schools attempting to leave more than an impression on our students, to be remembered for making a profound impact on their students' lives. Much has changed over the years to expand their role and force change on a profession that has been among the most respected in the world. As we address this expanded role, let's begin with a look back at the role of teachers then and now.

Successful schools in past years were characterized by the values taught to children at home. Students came to school with a purpose, a sense of direction, and respect for what education brings to their lives. Because children already understood why they were at school, teachers could immediately begin the teaching and learning process. Today, as illustrated in Figure 3.1, the absence of that very foundation has left principals, teachers, and schools in a reactionary mode.

Figure 3.1   How the Roles of Teachers Have Changed

New Realities of Teaching	
From	*To*
Teacher at the center	Testing at the center
Individualism	Cooperative learning
Teacher and book	Inquiry and practice
Students ready to learn	Reluctant learners
Teacher as clinician	Teacher as leader
Curriculum based	Standards driven
Classroom issues/concerns	Whole school concerns
Home	School

Teachers today are finding it more and more difficult to concentrate on teaching when there are so many other things to accomplish. Their role is expanded and they experience stress like never before; many are looking for a way out of the profession they once loved.

THE REALITIES OF TEACHING

There are more than two and a half million K–12 teachers working at almost 90,000 public schools in America. Teachers constitute 4% of the civilian workforce. There are twice as many teachers as registered nurses and five times as many teachers as lawyers (Ingersoll, 2001). Seventy-five percent of teachers are women, and the majority of those teachers have dependents (Ingersoll, 2001). Public school teaching has tradition-ally been a major avenue to the mid-

What are some of the posi-tive characteristics you saw in teachers as a child and what positive characteristics do you see now?

dle class for many people. Although there is a large volume of research on teachers and teaching, almost none of it examines the lives of teachers beyond the classroom or takes any account of the relationships between the workplace and other responsibilities, such as family.

Many scholars, as well as the public, believe that teaching is easy work that is compatible with family life. However, in recent years the demands of teaching have increased while the compensation of teachers, in relation to other professionals of comparable education, has decreased (Liu, Kardos, Kauffman, Peske, & Johnson, 2000). This has led to increased occupa-tional stress, difficulty balancing family and work, and an increase in attrition (i.e., leaving the profession). The rates of teacher turnover are higher now than ever before and higher than many other occupations. Although reports vary, most agree that 40%–50% of teachers leave the profession within the first five years of teaching (Ingersoll & Smith, 2003).

A full 45% of teacher attrition and 33% of teacher migra-tion (leaving one school for another) is credited to personal reasons such as pregnancy, child-rearing, and health problems (Ingersoll, 2001).

The expectations made of teachers are expanding. For at least two decades, advocates of teaching reforms, especially those focused on professionalism, have taken pride in a steady expansion of teachers' work roles and responsibilities. Today, teachers must be leaders in their schools and take on roles outside of the classroom, including the school's assessment systems, system delivery, and curriculum development. This new organizational system represents a dramatic shift in what is expected of them.

The image of the teacher as a "specialist" in a specific subject who stands alone in front of a classroom of students is still a reality today in some contexts, particularly at the secondary level. However, this perception of the role of teachers no longer matches the demands of teaching and educational needs of all of our students.

An education system that aims to offer a quality education for all its students should be able to count on teachers who are well trained and adequately compensated for their services. Further, teachers should be capable of following the evolving processes and structure of knowledge and have the necessary competencies to take into account the growing needs of our students and families at all levels that directly or indirectly affect our schools. We are suffering from a shortage of teachers, or at least teachers who are qualified in particular subject areas. There are numerous obstacles that limit the number of well-trained, competent teachers in classrooms, such as low wages, heavy workloads, large class sizes, limited prospects for advancement, student behavior problems, and lack of support from leaders.

Many systems are suffering from aging secondary teaching staff, which further accentuates the cultural distance between students and the teachers who are responsible for their engagement in the classroom and, ultimately, for their success in school. Moreover, many competent young people are taking higher revenue professional opportunities. Young people are now leaving the formal education system having lost the motivation to learn and the desire to emulate teachers and make this a professional choice.

When I asked a group of 900 high school students if they planned on entering the teaching profession, I was amazed when only four hands went up. Many students began shouting, "Oh no, I wouldn't deal with what teachers have to deal with," and others responded, "They don't make enough money."

In years past, there were many more high school graduates on their way to becoming the next generation of teachers than there are now. The future looked bright for them as they went off to colleges and universities to receive formal training to enter the world's most important profession. But now, times have changed, and most of today's students lack the drive to enter this important profession.

> **Why did you become an educator?**

Current teachers, too, seem to lack pride in their profession. Whereas, in the past, they would respond with pride when asked of their profession, now some teachers shy away from that question as if to say, please don't ask! Society does not look upon them as they do actors or lawyers. My grandmother and mother were teachers. Growing up, I was in awe of teachers because of their demeanor and presence, their intelligence and the way they carried themselves. They were powerful shapers of the future. I entered the profession of teaching because I believed in its purpose. I believe teachers are "called to teach." It is a deep calling similar to that of a pastor or priest. It seems odd that anyone would not understand and embrace this calling, as teaching is one of the most important marks we can leave on this world. But the demands that are being placed on our teachers are forcing us to reexamine the very core of our delivery system.

School systems and those in them are looking for ways to capture the essence of what was and is no longer present. As consultants, trainers, or staff developers come across students, teachers, parents, superintendents, school boards, and community members in our travels, conversations almost always turn to finding answers to many of our educational system's complex problems. Everyone wants a first-class, quality school system, but many are confused about how to create it in the face of demands from multiple entities.

As we explore these demands on our current delivery system, we offer the reader a look at some possible solutions. Creating top-ranked school systems requires more than hard work. Most of our teachers and administrators are already working hard. We need a better operating system that serves the needs of the very reason we're all in this—our students.

Successful Delivery Systems

Teachers need successful delivery systems to develop opportunities in which effective teaching and learning can take shape. One way of doing this is to shift the question from "*is* this student smart?" to "*how is* this student smart?"

When we focus on effective delivery systems and the benefits of these systems for students, we begin to create schools of quality. From experience, I have learned the power of students having a voice in a school environment, a voice that doesn't have to scream to be heard, but one that is respected and honored as much as any other voice.

Ninety percent of our problems in schools are caused by 10% of our student population. When we create schools that deliver the essential fifteen system deliverables (see below) to their students, we will begin to see this 10% reduced. The students causing the problems then become part of your management team, as demonstrated with the Gentlemen's Club in Chapter 1. They will begin informing you of what's about to happen before it happens. They will begin to feel a sense of belonging to a "family" and act accordingly.

The school system delivery (Figure 3.2) is an important and vital element of creating top-ranked schools. Collaboration between families, teachers, and schools creates a unified front that can seldom be broken. Developing these relationships can take time and energy that many schools are choosing not to expend, but they must expend it in order to combat the results of not doing so.

Figure 3.2   System Deliverables to Students

System Deliverables to Students

System should provide but not be limited to the following:

1. Opportunity
2. Accomplishment and success
3. Safe and secure environments
4. Quality teachers and administrators
5. Specialized programs that work
6. Relevant school and classroom experiences
7. Structure
8. Consistent rules and processes
9. Identification of dreams and aspirations
10. Identification and development of natural gifts
11. A plan to use those gifts
12. Essential skills
13. Empowerment
14. A safe haven (7.5 hours a day, Monday through Friday, more if necessary)
15. HOPE

TEACHER PERSONALITY TYPES

According to researcher James White, there are four types of teachers working with our students; each functions in totally different ways as they interact with each other and, more important, with students each day (White, 2003). As teachers become engaged in their workday, positive interaction with other teachers and students is one of the keys to producing highly effective schools. Some teachers are finding it more and more difficult to separate issues they have with students with issues they have with each other. The more we are able to understand the different personality types of those with whom we work, the better results we will begin to have in our schools.

The four types of teachers are:

1. Highly active. Highly active teachers are hard working, energetic team players. They're usually heads of committees or team leaders; they are connected with administration and others outside of the building. They believe that they are critical pieces of the puzzle, and they are usually correct. They serve on many committees and offer advice openly.

In the classroom, highly active teachers are engaging, and they use many different approaches to capture their students' attention. They will dress up in costume, sing, dance, or perform. These teachers make learning fun. The classroom is their stage.

2. Active. If we could hire active teachers in all of our schools, we would experience success at all levels. They are hard-working, healthy individuals who would rather give the team credit than take it for themselves. They understand why they do what they do and are willing to go the extra mile without complaining. They're willing to volunteer time and time again for the right cause, and in return they are highly respected by their administrators, other teachers, parents, and students.

In the classroom, active teachers deliver lessons that are well planned. They teach for understanding and will not stop until they are convinced that students grasp the concepts. The classroom is their factory.

3. Passive. Passive teachers are formerly active teachers who are now reserved and overly concerned about what others may define as "normal" issues. They will pose 20 questions about simple tasks and otherwise provide many challenges for administrators and team members.

In the classroom, passive teachers use worksheets to keep students busy. They will assign in-class reading when students complete written assignments to ensure that there is enough "busy work" to make time go by faster. This is not a very engaging classroom environment. The classroom is their holding cell.

4. Victim. The most difficult of the four, the victim teacher will provide challenges for everyone they come in contact with, including parents. Things never seem right for the victims and, according to their insight, things will never be right.

In the classroom, victims will write numerous office referrals to get rid of students whom they deem trouble-makers. They seldom make good connections with students and will spend an enormous amount of time off task while delving into conversations about unrelated material. The classroom is their therapist.

What kind of teacher are you? What kind of teachers do you want to work with in your school?

Understanding the differences between teacher types is at the core of creating top-ranked schools and classrooms. As we operate under increased demands, we have to do so with a high degree of quality among our staff. Moreover, we have to develop a deeper understanding of those around us and make a commitment not only to bring our best stuff every day, but also to challenge others to bring theirs.

Teaching is not just the transmission of facts and skills; it is the unique ability to help our students grasp concepts and develop a higher order of thinking that will enable them to rise to the high expectations established for them. Since the 1980s, critics of public education have argued that many American students do not possess the depth of knowledge or skills to assure personal life success or national economic competitiveness. One major concern has always been the inability of our students to engage in complex problem-solving activities and to apply school knowledge and skills to real-life problems. But it should not be surprising to us that our students fail to meet our expectations, because the traditional measures of school outcomes—standardized achievement tests—have not required the application of knowledge in new settings.

What schools and teachers face is a fundamental redefinition of what it means to be a student or a teacher and what it means to teach and learn. Educators are confronting a paradigm shift that is being driven by the increasing demands of the current educational system. High dropout rates, low skill and knowledge levels among many students, low levels of student engagement in student work, and poor comparisons to other systems suggest that the current system is weak and inappropriate. The task confronting all of us as we seek to better our schools and learning opportunities for our students is to learn to work with our students and the subject matter in fundamentally different ways. It is apparent that many of our teachers are caught in the midst of a change for which they may not have been professionally prepared. Many teachers were educated in classrooms in which the role of the student was to memorize information, and then they were tested on their ability to repeat tasks or exchange the information given to them. That model is no longer enough, and our beliefs about how schools should be are causing the tension and disappointment as they clash with new expectations of what schools should accomplish.

How to Avoid Blind Spots

In order for us to move forward, we must do so united with a common belief system. If all children can learn, then we must answer the central question, "Why aren't they learning?" We create "blind spots" when we are not honest in our appraisal of what we truly feel about students—about where they live, who their parents are, their socioeconomic status or, more important, their ability to learn. Because we want to avoid offending anyone, we create these blind spots that make it increasingly difficult to reach students who become disconnected for some reason along the way. Through no fault of their own, they encounter a teacher or administrator who confirms for them what they perceive from their homes—that nobody really cares.

In successful schools, effective team members are creating an environment where having different opinions is accepted and in some cases respected. The essence of what we do and who we are is dependent on our ability to be different, have opposing viewpoints, and disagree, but not be disagreeable. Our acceptance of each other's backgrounds and cultures aids our acceptance of our students' differing backgrounds and cultures. But when

ଓ ଓ

What are your blind spots?

we reveal what we think others will agree with or accept instead of what we truly believe, we create blind spots, and in the end, our students suffer. As they say, "you're not being real." That is what our students desire and need: adults who are "real."

Current research, while building on findings indicating the vital role teachers play in stimulating learning, also focuses on the role of the student. It recognizes that students do not merely passively receive or copy input from teachers, but instead actively mediate it by trying to make sense of it and to relate it to what they already know or think they know about the topic. Thus, students develop new knowledge through their own process of construction. In order to get beyond rote memorization to achieve understanding of a subject, they need to develop and integrate a network of associations linking new input to preexisting knowledge, beliefs, and experiences. As the role of teachers continues to expand, the most important factor to understand is that teaching involves inducing conceptual changes in students, not merely infusing knowledge in a vacuum.

In an attempt to achieve coverage of as much material as possible in the classroom, schools have opted for speed and efficiency, thereby depriving students of the important steps that lead to deep personal understanding and the grasping of concepts that can and should be transferred from one subject or level to the next.

KNOWLEDGE WORK

In their expanded role, teachers must remember that the real work of schools is knowledge work:

Figure 3.3   Knowledge Work

- Knowledge of what
- Knowledge of why
- Knowledge of how to
- Knowledge of when to
- Knowledge of others
- Knowledge of self

There are no magic solutions when it comes to creating success in our schools and classrooms (Peters, 2001). But there are approaches that put us a little closer to meeting our goals and realizing our vision. For example, how we treat students and each other can introduce a climate of respect and lead to positive change. How students are taught (not always teacher-centered lectures) and what they are taught (curriculum must be meaningful and relevant) can lead to academic recovery for many who have been turned off to teachers and learning. The knowledge we possess of what, why, how to, and when to, as it pertains to all learners, will provide a framework for exciting teaching and learning opportunities that can be sustained over time.

The struggle for reform in education can be understood as a challenge to the existing knowledge system. Our beliefs about the nature of knowledge will always influence the roles, rules, and responsibilities of our schools. Beliefs about knowledge are revealed in the way curriculum is organized, instruction is conducted, and assessment occurs.

Classroom experiences for today's students must be stimulating and relevant in order for teachers to capture their attention. Students must also understand the whys and hows of the knowledge teachers are transferring to them or encouraging them to gain on their own. Teaching for understanding has become a prerequisite for those in our profession who not only wish to survive, but also wish to make more than a difference in the life of each student.

Transforming low-performing schools and sustaining efforts have produced a number of successful principles and practices that are in use around the country today. For example, Tricia McManus and her team of dedicated teachers at Just Elementary School in Tampa, Florida are approaching their success with excitement and motivation as many of the early indicators suggest they are on the right path of transforming their low-achieving school and making it a model for others.

In addition to the five common elements listed below, Just Elementary has adopted the slogan "Together We Can"; their prescription for transformation includes proposing dedicated teamwork, strong and confident leadership, a focused mission and vision, a relevant curriculum, and a strong belief in all students.

There are five common elements that have emerged:

- The teacher's role is to develop strategies that will support and respond to students' learning, not just to present information.
- The content is organized around a set of relevant themes.
- The teacher creates a social environment in the classroom in which dialogue promotes deeper understanding.
- The students' role is to actively make sense and construct meaning from the knowledge and facts presented.
- Classroom instruction features authentic tasks that call for problem solving and critical thinking, not memorization or reproduction.

Embedded in these five principles is an approach to offset the many demands placed on our teachers. Teachers should constantly rely on the key principle of "understanding rather than coverage."

The constant and numerous demands placed on our teachers have caused a tremendous amount of frustration and fear that we may never retrieve the honor our profession once held. As the "news flash" for this chapter, I offer you the following to process: **Our children are depending on you to restore hope to their unfortunate lives, and many of them believe you are their last hope.** We cannot continue to concentrate on the expanded role of teaching. We have to do what others before us have done in times of adversity. Let us now roll up our sleeves, dig deep down in our souls, and teach like we mean it every day, ALL day, so that no more students leave our presence unprepared to meet the demands of the next level. Further, let us commit ourselves to caring so much that failure is erased, the achievement gap is eliminated, and our society regains the most valuable asset it has ever known—an educated populace.

CHAPTER SUMMARY

In years past, teachers prepared lessons to deliver to students who, for the most part, came to school ready to learn. Parent support was at an all-time high, and administrators were available to appropriately handle issues that arose outside of teaching.

Today, the new realities of teaching require school leaders and teachers to employ a much different delivery system for success. From understanding the "new student" and avoiding blind spots, to understanding the "new teacher" and assembling an effective team, this chapter emphasized the importance of understanding that education is now knowledge work—knowledge of what, what for, how to, and when.

Chapter 4 poses a critical question, "If all students can learn, then why aren't they learning?" and then proceeds to explain why schools operate the way they do. The chapter introduces teaching and learning styles, not to completely define them, but to explain how each affects learning.

4

If "All Children Can Learn," Then Why Aren't They Learning?

The greatest gift we can give a child is hope.

By the end of this chapter, in order to bring your best stuff every day, you should understand the following:

- Why Schools Operate Like They Do
- Learning Styles
- Teaching Styles
- How Learning Styles and Teaching Styles Affect Learning
- All Children Can Learn

I often ask myself the question, "If all children can learn, then why aren't they learning?" This seems to be a fair and logical question at a critical time in our society. If our country shares the belief that all children can learn, what drives it and how is it actually taking shape in our classrooms? The purpose of this chapter is to challenge educators all over the world to be honest about their belief systems. If we are to make a serious effort at closing the achievement gap in our districts, we must come to terms with our current philosophies and beliefs.

Our underlying belief system holds the key to unlocking some of the mystery surrounding this question. As a child growing up in the public school system, I always sensed that my teachers sincerely believed that I could master the material they presented to us. What stood out for me was the fact that they were excited about delivering it in such a way that we could grasp the concepts and then apply them in other situations. Teachers treated all of us the same way, and we believed that teachers had high expectations for each of us.

In contrast, today's schools and classrooms are filled with students who receive different messages from teachers about their promise as students and what is expected of them. Students revealed in interviews for another project that they clearly felt a different set of expectations applied to them and to some of their classmates. When asked why they had this impression, many responded, "You just know." That was a very powerful statement. Students have an innate ability, almost a sixth sense, to discern what others think about them. They know when someone truly cares or when they are being led astray by poor learning conditions and low expectations. Many of our students are being led astray when not given the same opportunities to learn under the same conditions as others.

Do you believe that all children can learn?

School mission statements attempt to highlight these opportunities in their efforts to capture the essence of the school. Over time, mission statements, if developed properly, can serve as a driving force to deliver what schools have collaboratively identified as critical linkages to success.

Moreover, a mission is a direction one chooses to take to bring about a desired outcome. However, mission statements written without the benefit of collaboration are just paragraphs of words that sound good but have very little substance when it comes to outcomes and measurable results.

One such mission statement is written below:

Figure 4.1   An Example of a High School Mission Statement

"Hawkins High School is a community with a passion for learning, dedicated to educational excellence for all students and staff. We are committed to high standards and exceeding our comfortable limits. We will teach our students, using a collaborative approach to learning and a differentiating instructional approach while producing global and productive members of society."

Anyone who reads the above might walk away feeling a sense of direction, but the critical question is, do the teachers, students, parents, and support staff members buy into this? Do they even remember what it says? When I asked a group of 7,000 teachers how many of them knew their mission statement, only 33 actually even knew what it said. That is unacceptable if we want to provide a world-class, quality education to all of our students.

Every year, millions of diverse six- to eighteen-year-olds enroll in our nation's schools. They are forming attitudes, beliefs, and values that will largely affect their lives as adults. They deserve schools that support

Does your school have a mission or vision statement? Do you know it?

them fully during each phase of life. As we attempt to provide quality for all learners, we must collaborate at every level and take ownership of all of our students. High-school teachers have to stop blaming middle-school teachers, middle-school teachers have to stop blaming elementary teachers, and elementary teachers have to stop blaming the home. Homes are sending us the best they have. It is critical that we accept the challenge before us and begin to find solutions to save this generation of learners.

WHY SCHOOLS OPERATE LIKE THEY DO

Currently, we operate an education system that dates back to the 1950s (Dolan, 1993). At that time, our country prepared some workers for factory jobs and others to work in the fields. School systems were built then to cater to the mentality of mass production. This system was efficient and turned out students who were ready to take on the demands of an industrial society.

Today, as we grapple with instant information in a high-tech world, the 1950s are a distant memory. Why, then, are we still attempting to educate students as if we're preparing them for a life of machine or assembly line work? To say our scholastic curriculum offering is outmoded is putting it mildly. As we attempt to answer the question this chapter poses, we must begin by stating that today's students need to learn skills that will help them in today's job market. The school system should teach students to make decisions on their own, work well with others, and decipher vast amounts of information.

How do we do it? First, we need to understand how our students learn. Second, we need to understand how we teach. Third, we need to provide relevant learning experiences to our students that will help them make sense of the world we live in.

LEARNING STYLES

In order to be an effective educator, it is important to understand different learning styles as defined in the theory of multiple intelligences (Gardner, 1983).

Visual

Those who have a visual learning style learn best if a major component of the material or lesson being taught is something they can see or watch. They work best with written material and instructions. They take in material or information and translate it into and store it as pictures in their brains. These learners are usually well organized, neat, and on time. In the classroom, visual learners are attentive, as they don't wish to miss anything. Many visual learners sit in the front of the classroom. Unnecessary movements can distract them.

Careers that suit the visual learner include the following:

- Executive positions
- Architects
- Engineers
- Surgeons
- Artists

Auditory

Those who have an auditory learning style learn best if there is an oral component to the material being learned. Verbal instructions and face-to-face instruction work best for these learners. They filter the information they hear and store the relevant data but don't necessarily form pictures around it as visual learners do. When problem solving, auditory learners prefer to talk it out, and they may use terms or phrases that relate to how they learn, such as, "I hear you."

Careers that suit the auditory learner include the following:

- Pathologists
- Disc jockeys
- Musicians
- Producers

In the classroom, these students attempt to avoid sitting next to talkers so they can be sure to hear the teacher. Unnecessary noise can be a distraction for auditory learners.

Kinesthetic

Those who have a kinesthetic or tactile learning style learn best when they can touch or feel what they are learning about. The use of their body and feelings is very important to these learners. Hands-on projects work best for them. Kinesthetic learners do not always have a great sense of order in their daily routines. They often live for the moment and do not have a vision for the future. They often speak in terms of feelings, such as statements to the effect of "I feel that. . . ." Kinesthetic learners tend to move around while attempting to solve a problem, so it is critical for those teaching this type of student to realize what is occurring and, more important, why it is happening.

Careers that suit the kinesthetic learner include the following:

- Anything that involves movement
- Dancer
- Acting
- Athletics
- Construction

In the classroom, these students will require assistance with outlining the lesson to aid understanding of main ideas. They are impulsive and many times will require the teacher to redirect their learning throughout the day. Because they tend to move around while trying to solve a problem, learning in their own space will allow for their desired movement.

It is important to note that the learning styles theory implies that how much individuals learn has more to do with whether the educational experience is geared toward their particular style of learning than with whether the student is "smart." Moreover, as I stated in Chapter 3, teachers should never ask, "*is* this student smart?" but rather, "*how is* this student smart?"

Understanding of different learning styles creates a different mind-set for teachers. The energy spent in the classroom answering the question, "how is this student smart?" will go a long way toward cultivating a culture that breeds success for all learners in the class—much further than the energy that comes from the question we've been asking for years, "is this student smart?"

TEACHING STYLES

Understanding how students learn is one step in the right direction of determining how teachers teach (Jackson, 1986). The second step is understanding our style of teaching and determining how to make a con-

What percentages of the students in your classroom are visual, auditory, or kinesthetic learners?

nection between teaching and learning styles so that we can produce desirable outcomes in the classroom.

There are four main teaching styles:

- Formal Authority
- Facilitator
- Demonstrator
- Delegator

Formal Authority

This teaching style is generally teacher-centered. Teachers who have a formal teaching style focus mainly on content. They feel responsible for providing and controlling the flow of the content, and they think that the student's task is to receive it.

Formal authority teachers are less concerned with building relationships with their students and more concerned with a give-and-take scenario in their classroom—meaning that the teacher gives and the student receives! "Sage on the stage" is their model.

Facilitator

This teaching style emphasizes student-centered learning, and it places much more responsibility on the students to take the initiative for meeting the demands of various learning tasks. This type of teaching style works best for students who are comfortable with self-directed learning and can work independently or collaborate with other students with equal comfort. Facilitators usually assign group activities that necessitate active learning, student collaboration, and problem solving. Teachers who facilitate must create relationships with their students first in order to create buy-in. Facilitator-led classrooms often have a sense of family. Facilitators design learning situations and activities that require students to process and then apply their content knowledge in creative ways.

Demonstrator

These teachers act as role models by demonstrating skills and knowledge and then as coaches in helping students develop and apply them. Demonstrators tend to run teacher-centered classrooms. They are interested in encouraging student participation and will adapt their presentation to include various learning styles. They expect students to take responsibility for their learning and encourage them to ask for help when they need it.

Delegator

Teachers with this teaching style place a great deal of control and responsibility for learning on individuals or groups of students. They will often give students a choice about designing and implementing their own lessons and class projects. Delegators act in a consultant role to their students and believe in their ability to work effectively in groups. The effectiveness of this classroom largely depends on the creation of a culture of self-directed learners. Behavior problems have no place in this classroom. However, those students who thrive on being social with other students often find success in classrooms with teachers who operate under this style.

How Learning Styles and Teaching Styles Affect Learning

Whole-brain teaching is an instructional approach derived from neurolinguistic descriptions of the function of the brain's left and right hemispheres (Buzan, 1976). In the integrated brain, the functions of one hemisphere are immediately available to the other, producing a more balanced use of language. Whole-brain teaching emphasizes active learning, in which the student makes connections tapping both hemispheres. Thus, imaging—being able to "see" what is being taught—is seen as the basis for comprehension.

> ⋙ ⋘
>
> **What type of teaching style do you demonstrate in the classroom?**

Knowledge is integrated in the center of classrooms that share values, beliefs, languages, and ways of doing things. We must create schools and classrooms that empower ALL of our learners to have a sense of belonging to something that stands for something.

To reach all learners, teachers should concentrate on the following areas.

- **Developing curriculum**. Teachers must place special emphasis on imagination, intuition, and feeling, in addition to the traditional skills and standards of analysis, reason, and problem solving. Content that is relevant and meaningful is critical in order to teach this generation of learners.

- **Delivering instruction**. Instruction must be designed to connect with all learning styles, using various combinations of reflection, experience, and experimentation. Today's students truly appreciate visuals, music, sounds, movement, and, of course, interactive conversations, and teachers should incorporate them into daily classroom instruction.

- **Doing assessments**. A variety of assessment techniques should be employed, focusing on the development of the whole-brain capacity and each of the different learning styles.

ALL CHILDREN CAN LEARN

We have created a separation of learners in our schools by our very own inability to see beyond the material aspects of our new society and socioeconomic status. Additionally, we have carved a street from our cultural exposure that only those with similar experiences travel on. The very mention of our inability to have the same expectations for students who didn't grow up as we did stirs emotions beyond the "comfort zone" many educators have. For us to believe that all students can learn, we must first grapple with our personal belief systems.

Mastery learning proposes that all children can learn when provided with the appropriate learning conditions in the classroom. Academic success only comes to students whose other developmental needs have also been met. The appropriate learning conditions in this new classroom must include three critical elements, depicted in Figure 4.2, that open the door for everything else to take shape and that must be sustained to ensure ongoing success.

Figure 4.2   How All Children Can Learn

- Familiarity: Empowering all students to become familiar with each other, surroundings, rules, procedures, and vision.
- Comfort: Enabling all students to become comfortable with teacher, school, and other students.
- Trust: The very core of our ability to produce students who will be able to take their rightful place in this world.

Contemporary society presents different challenges from those we faced decades ago. Although the traditional school functions—acquiring fundamental knowledge, teaching the tools of citizenship, and sharing our national heritage—remain valid, achieving these functions today and meeting the academic needs of our students requires more than good teachers and leaders. This effort requires GREAT teachers and leaders who understand the spirit of ALL of our students, leaders who will always remember that the more appropriate question to ask ourselves is, "how is this student smart?"

How is each student in your classroom smart?

Successful schools where ALL students can learn are characterized by a culture that includes but is not limited to the following:

- **Courageous leadership**. Leaders are confidently stepping out of the box and creating opportunities for teachers, staff, and students. When they involve others and view themselves as the provider of resources, other team members are encouraged to give 100% because they feel the synergy.
- **A shared vision that guides decisions**. Seeing the desired outcome is always one of the keys to achieving it. Successful schools in which leaders are able to articulate a clear vision and obtain buy-in from at least 80% of those working with them are reaping rewards for students (Black, 1994).
- **A safe, clean, and secure environment**. Students and staff alike ranked this as the most important of all areas if they are going to cultivate an effective climate and culture for success in their school (Peters, 2006).
- **Teachers and students engaged in active learning**. The creation of partnerships between administrators, teachers, and students is paying big dividends in the area of student learning. Modeling behavior you expect creates a win-win situation for all involved.
- **An adult advocate for every student**. Whereas providing a clean, safe, and secure environment ranks highest, the presence of an adult advocate for each student is not very far behind as one of the most critical needs for

schools to fulfill. Once created, this relationship provides the framework for students to have hope again. Trust is built over time through these connections. Through these relationships, school becomes an important place for many students.

- **Family, community, and business partnerships**. I define synergy as "the efforts of more than one far outweigh the efforts of one." Many schools now making their mark in student achievement are using the slogan "Together We Can," as described in Chapter 3. Securing these partnerships and sustaining them over time will produce results.
- **Teachers who truly care about the whole student**. Teachers often share stories of restoring hope to students they found hard to reach. At the core of their success is the connection to the whole student. When students ask, "Do you know enough about me to teach me?" many teachers are responding with an unequivocal "YES!"
- **High expectations for every student and every adult**. Nobody rises to low expectations! Adults and students respond to the expectations set forth for them. One of the issues we face in public education today is the simple fact that our problem is not that our students aren't rising to our expectations—the problem is that they are. We must have high expectations at all times for every student and every adult working with our students.

Therefore, these schools must provide the following:

- Schoolwide efforts that ensure wellness and safety become integral parts of its mission
- Curriculum that is relevant, challenging, exploratory, and integrative
- Effective guidance and support
- Daily operating systems that are consistent, effective, and fair

- Multiple learning and teaching approaches that respond to diversity
- Assessment and evaluative processes that promote achievement

The foundation of successful schools where ALL students can learn is driven by the spirit of intent. **Success is the only option!**

Chapter Summary

Schools face enough difficulty that they shouldn't have to face more when students sit in the classroom prepared to receive instruction from their teacher. Students have different learning styles, just as teachers have different teaching styles. When teachers realize this, they greatly increase the chances of success because they can deliver instruction and material to students in a manner they can better process and understand. If a teacher can make this match work, it has a positive effect on student learning.

Chapter 5 provides the readers with insight into results that are sometimes hidden or overshadowed by what we determine to be the more important outcomes for student and school success. Through providing rewards for students and developing school partnerships, some schools are beginning to understand there is also value in measuring results we overlook.

5

Measuring Results That Count

Effective assessment for learners involves more than adopting new assessment strategies. It involves rethinking the way curriculum, instruction, and assessment work together to improve student learning.

By the end of this chapter, in order to bring your best stuff every day, you should understand the following:

- How to Reward Students
- School Partnerships and Relationships

In the last 40 years, layer upon layer of tests have been added so that we now have districtwide, statewide, national, and international assessment programs operating simultaneously (Stiggins, 2002).

On January 8, 2002, President Bush signed the No Child Left Behind Act, which required more standardized tests of every student in mathematics and reading every year in

Grades three through eight. Presently, our school systems are doing everything possible to live up to the standards set forth in that legislation, but are finding it difficult to do so without enough funding.

Research indicates that it is important to include a variety of assessments that go beyond paper and pencil tests without excluding traditional forms of assessment (Leon & Elias, 1998). Formative assessment has always played a pivotal role in student learning when it is appropriately included in the classroom. That is, given certain conditions, formative assessment makes a significant difference in student achievement, particularly for low-achieving students. One specific strategy is having teachers give their students frequent short quizzes instead of infrequent long tests as a measure of checking certain levels of knowledge. In order to support higher levels of learning for ALL students, we must begin to view the whole student and not create tunnel vision for our teachers as they embark on the never-ending journey of reaching a certain page number by a certain date only to find out that the majority of their students haven't learned what they were supposed to learn.

Schools that believe that success builds success will begin making progress toward becoming quality schools, and they must celebrate small successes along the way by measuring results that count—results that cannot be quantitatively measured, such as the attitude of a student improving or the confidence of a new teacher improving and enabling him or her to deliver instruction better. Measuring results that count does not underestimate the importance of formal assessments or their ability to assist in determining

What is a small success you have witnessed in your school?

levels of achievement. Simply put, its targets are those students who have failed standardized assessment tests all of their young lives and have no desire to accommodate them further. In order to get this specific group of students to become an active part of this critical measurement of their success, we must become creative in our approach.

REWARDING STUDENTS

Working with an elementary school in South Carolina recently gave my consulting group an opportunity to let students reluctant about testing become active members in a drive to change the public perception of their school. Alongside a courageous leader and a group of committed teachers, we examined the assessment data and realized that a major part of the lower than expected test scores was not a result of students being unable to perform but a result of students being absent on testing days.

As the testing period approached, one of the ideas we gave them was to issue a promise: all students who achieved perfect attendance for the six days of testing would receive a new bicycle. This was a big deal, as most of the students in this school had never owned a new bicycle. The excitement was unreal. Testing began and on the first day, not one student in the testing grades was absent.

Day two: 100% attendance.

Day three: 100% attendance.

Day four: 100% attendance.

Day five: 100% attendance.

Day six: 100% attendance.

Parents would call the front office of the school from the parking lot saying, "Don't mark my child absent, we're right here in the parking lot." Students were changing out of their pajamas in that school parking lot!

Along with a committed group of business partners, the school was able to make good on its promise to the students who came through in such a big way. The school purchased more than 100 brand-new bicycles and had them delivered to the school after testing ended. They were lined up down the hallway in spectacular fashion, and students were on top of the world that day as they came face to face with the combination of hard work and reward!

It's no coincidence that test scores for this school soared, and they were recently named both a State and National Blue Ribbon School. Not all schools can provide bicycles, but this example is one of the many ways schools can select to measure results that count.

—————— ✑ ✑ ——————

What has your school done to reward students?

Faculty members, too, react positively to small rewards. Figure 5.1 contains other tips for rewarding students and faculty.

Figure 5.1   Tips for Rewarding Students and Faculty

- **Celebrate "small" successes**. Even a 2% increase in attendance is worthy of celebrating. Remember, success breeds success. For example, serve food after a standard faculty meeting and invite someone from the central office to come in to say thank you to the staff for their efforts. Give certificates of appreciation and a gift certificate to all staff members who had perfect attendance this month.
- **Communicate more with students**. Allow their voices to be heard. Many times students have the answers to questions with which we struggle. For example, add student leaders to your school improvement team or comparable committee and allow them to bring their perspective to the table.
- **Measure declining trends such as referrals to the office**. As part of regular meetings, keep staff abreast of declining trends such as in-school suspensions, out-of-school suspensions, expulsions, teacher absences, and student absences. The entire staff should be knowledgeable about using data to make informed decisions. In order to accomplish this, important data has to be disaggregated and used.
- **Pay closer attention to the content of meetings.** The more you move in the direction of instruction becoming the topic of discussion at meetings, the more success you will experience with every learner in your school. For example, appoint a person just as you would a timekeeper in a meeting to keep discussion moving along the right path.

- **Encourage active learning**. Leaders, teachers, students, and homes should become one small learning community. The success of this venture will depend on it being a core element embedded in the school's vision. For example, as a staff, select a book to read and study together. Book studies are becoming a good way for schools to learn together in a supportive way.
- **Keep track of student engagement**. Today's leaders must make it a priority to observe instruction on a daily basis to determine the level of student engagement, teacher preparation, and instructional delivery. For example, place a folder outside of each classroom door (like at a doctor's examining room) and keep a record of your visits to that classroom in it.
- **Monitor teacher and staff morale**. Keep a finger on the pulse of what the adults in the building are feeling at all times. Validation and affirmation are critical links to the success of schools. As I discussed in Chapter 1, handwrite notes to your teachers and support staff members weekly thanking them for their time, efforts, and passion. This will go a long way toward creating communities of caring and highly successful schools for all learners.

As we set out to measure results that count, we must keep in mind that every student is unique in his or her own way and has a specific culture and personal background, not to mention a different array of learning styles, interests, talents, and skills. Chapter 4 explained that no single teaching method would work for every student we encounter. In fact, no single teaching method will work for any one student every day. Research suggests that using varied and appropriate strategies and teaching has a positive effect on student learning (Cawelti, 1995; Epstein & Mac Iver, 1992; Russell, 1997). Given the need for variety in teaching and learning approaches, what does work for ALL learners? According to research, students learn best when they form a partnership with their teachers and together they do the following:

- Establish a classroom environment in which students and teachers understand the cultural backgrounds represented in the classroom, communicate acceptance and positive attitudes about cultural diversity, and build on this diversity through day-to-day teaching and learning activities to promote pride and motivation (Gay, 2000; Shumow & Harris, 1998; Villegas & Lucas, 2002).

- Pay attention to learning styles (Dunn & Dunn, 1978, 1987) as student strengths to be built on and as justification for using a variety of teaching methods (Rosenshine, 1971).
- Connect new learning to prior knowledge and understanding (Bruning, Schraw, & Ronning, 1999).
- Engage in hands-on activities in meaningful contexts.
- Draw on the community as a resource for learning.
- Decide what and how to study, because students learn best when they have some control over their learning (Beane, 1997; Tomlinson, 1999; Wiggins & McTighe, 1998).
- Enhance and accommodate diverse skills, interests, abilities, and talents (Tomlinson, 1999).

When teaching and learning approaches are varied, given the diversity of ALL types of learners, there is a greater likelihood for student success—whether it's academic, social, or personal—when these approaches recognize and address students' needs, interests, and talents. While we're measuring results that count, we should note that our students have many concerns about matters that lie outside the parameters of the academic curriculum and need opportunities to share or discuss these with one another and with adults they have grown to trust.

Academic success increases markedly when students' affective needs are met. Therefore, all adults in our schools should view themselves as advocates, mentors, and advisors. The concept of advocacy is truly fundamental to every school's success and should be embedded in every aspect of its culture. The attitude of caring that translates into action when adults become responsive to the general and specific needs of ALL students will produce results that at times cannot be measured quantitatively.

The recognition that students learn differently and have different learning experiences and develop at varying rates makes it imperative that we change the way we educate them. Schools must begin this process by setting as their number one priority the sustaining of their efforts over time. Band-Aid approaches have been used for many years and have proved to be effective at only delaying the inevitable.

Our educational system and schools must create learning environments that provide ALL students an opportunity to learn basic skills that apply to real-life situations, proceed at a rate that is achievable for them, make no unfair comparisons with the progress of others, ensure positive reinforcement, and provide curriculum, instruction, and assessment procedures that reflect the many different ways students process information and learn.

SCHOOL PARTNERSHIPS

The true measure of successful schools is rooted in the human relationships at the school and includes parents or guardians and families, teachers, students, community members, the school board, the principal, and the district office.

Parents or Guardian and Families

It is imperative for educators to involve parents because they are an integral part of the school. They should also be kept well informed of all school activities and relevant news.

Parents are encouraged to be involved and supportive. For example, parents can now be notified if their child is absent on the day they are absent via telephone recording software. Monthly newsletters that are written with today's parent in mind are being used as a tool to keep parents informed of important dates and events involving their children. Computer software is now available to allow parents to check their children's homework assignments and grades. In addition, some schools are encouraging their teachers to use e-mail as an effective communication tool to keep parents informed and involved.

Teachers

Teachers are the real role models for our students and are brokers of information. Not only must teachers instruct, facilitate, coach, and guide our students through a process of discovery, they should celebrate accomplishments as they occur. Teachers provide more than just content to students; they are sometimes regarded as family to many of our students. Great teachers are America's true heroes. Gale Owens, a seventh-grade social studies teacher at Mauldin Middle School, says she was "born to teach." As she recalls, "I have always wanted to teach, even when I was a little girl." Doing whatever it takes for her students to succeed, "Mrs. O," as her students affectionately call her, continues to spend money out of her pocket to enable students who are less fortunate to have materials that are necessities in school. Further, she believes all of her students can and will be successful. She refuses to allow them to fail. Over time, she has proved that when students are given a chance in a culture of caring and trust, miracles happen.

Mrs. O is a hero!

Community Members

Community resources come in many forms. For example, some community members (successful business owners, city council members, politicians, doctors, lawyers, etc.) are former students who actually attended public school and could serve as positive role models to students in need of this influence. Their success can provide a wonderful example of the importance of education. Business and community members are stakeholders in the educational process and should be valued.

Students

Students must develop a true sense of belonging and caring about others and must respect one another as unique individuals. As active participants in the learning process, they must have many opportunities to have a say about the process. Students should understand the vision of the school and expectations about behavior and the learning process. They can also be great additions to school management teams and participate in the classroom environment as peer coaches in cooperative learning activities. School improvement teams are beginning to include student leaders as members who are being trained to serve as liaisons between fellow students, administrators, and teachers.

School Board and District Office

The school board and district office provide support and encouragement to school-level personnel. The school board should encourage each school in their district to become self-reliant, independent, and unique, yet still remain a part of a district team concept. In many school districts, school board members are assigned to specific schools, attend PTA meetings, and attend select faculty meetings as a way of increasing their knowledge of what's actually happening in the school and making themselves available to the teachers working on the front line.

Who are the heroes or role models in your school? What qualities do these individuals possess?

Being a proponent of the student as customer, the combination of all the partnerships should be more than enough for us to begin engineering education reform at its highest level while preparing for yet another generation of learners to come. **As we continue to embrace high-stakes testing, accountability, and the need for data-driven decisions, let us remember that our greatest accomplishment as educators**

is to be sure there is a teacher in every classroom, every day, ensuring that our students are learning and growing and, more important, feeling like human beings. This measurement also counts!

CHAPTER SUMMARY

In an era of high-stakes testing and accountability, educators are finding themselves frustrated with results that are not meeting their expectations. At the same time, there are schools that are accomplishing some amazing things with students who are supposedly hard to reach. They are getting results through various means, one of which is rewarding their students and teachers for obtaining incremental success.

Chapter 6 introduces the reader to the concept of creating #1 classrooms in which student engagement can be found at its highest level on a consistent basis. #1 classrooms have #1 teachers who cultivate a special culture and climate that sends this message to each student: "I care too much about you to ever allow you to fail."

6

Creating #1 Classrooms

#1 classrooms are grounded in the understanding that ALL learners are capable of far more than adults often assume.

By the end of this chapter, in order to bring your best stuff every day, you should understand the following:

- Your Educational Vision
- The Top 10 Requirements for #1 Classrooms
- Creating Effective Classrooms for All Learners
- #1 Classroom Teachers
- Managing the Classroom Climate

Successful classrooms are characterized by the active engagement of students and teachers. Teachers in these classrooms hold and act on high expectations for themselves and for ALL of their students. Likewise, students hold themselves and their teachers to equally high expectations. Teachers in #1 classrooms convey this by personal examples and gestures, but more important, by their attitudes.

In an attempt to achieve high academic achievement for every student, we must understand that it requires much more than gaining an adequate score on a standardized test. It means empowering students to learn by helping them develop initiative and responsibility for their learning.

We want to lay the foundation for creating a #1 classroom in which students do the following:

Figure 6.1   Goals for Creating a #1 Classroom

Students . . .
- Become partners in their learning
- Learn in a respectful, productive, positive atmosphere
- Are encouraged to share their thoughts, difficulties, successes, and dreams
- Recognize and respect their own culture and those of others
- Have opportunities to explain, clarify, expand on, or question
- Receive honest, timely, and respectful feedback about their work
- Recognize their own areas of strength in thinking and learning
- Identify their dreams, aspirations, and natural gifts
- Receive direction and vehicles for future success
- Receive instruction from amazing teachers

YOUR EDUCATIONAL VISION

In order to guide their behavior in class, you should reflect on your vision or style for teaching as well as your expectations of yourself and each student. It is a given that many students will be from diverse backgrounds and learn in different ways. Staying connected to your role as teacher and the vision and goals you have set for yourself will keep you balanced as you combat issues that arise out of our new societal ills.

In an article called "The Power of Self-Connections," Dr. Pamela Gerloff (1998) refers to the connection that educators need with themselves to work more effectively with students: "In each of us there is a space or state of awareness where we feel completely safe, protected and content. It is from this space of awareness that our unique life purpose, our destiny arises" (p. 151).

What is your personal educational vision?

The majority of people who teach do so from their heart and give everything they have to ensure that their students' lives are richer when they leave the classroom. However, this is becoming a task that more and more teachers are finding difficult to accomplish. Teachers who wish to reach and teach all learners must create an environment in which students can achieve the awareness Gerloff describes.

Imagine the thousands of students who never have a chance to understand their unique purpose in life or discover their destiny because they were not fortunate enough to have that special teacher or attend that special school that fostered the environment of trust or feeling of safety and contentment. Students today have many talents and gifts roaring to be released in the right environment, orchestrated by a caring adult with whom they've developed a healthy mutual respect. How a student feels becomes a critical factor in establishing a #1 classroom environment that breeds success for ALL learners. Teachers in these classrooms understand that relationships come before books and test results. They have a unique ability to offer their students a reprieve from the things in their lives that cause them pain and suffering. They create a classroom that becomes their students' second home, and some students come to desire it more than their first.

Once the foundation of the appropriate relationship is laid, effective teaching and learning can take place in this environment through effective partnerships, as discussed in Chapter 5.

But what defines a #1 classroom?

TOP 10 REQUIREMENTS FOR #1 CLASSROOMS

One. Classrooms must have teachers who remember why they became teachers. #1 classrooms have teachers who are driven by their purpose. The spark that was there when they first started teaching is still their driving force. If you've never been on fire, it's impossible to burn out. These teachers are on fire for the success of their students every day.

Two. Students must be treated as consumers of knowledge. Thirty-second television commercials, music videos, instant messaging, blogging, and computer games have our students waiting to be "sold" on a product. We must use this as an advantage to help them attain an appreciation for knowledge by delivering it in exciting and meaningful ways.

Three. Educators must always be nurturing and caring and provide a clean and safe environment. Students should feel a sense of community the moment they enter the school doors. Adults who deliver well-prepared lessons consistently and enforce policies and procedures fairly will seal this requirement. Both adults and students appreciate a clean and safe environment.

Four. Educators must be respectful of ALL students, regardless of race, size, socioeconomic status, or learning ability. Reciprocal respect and unconditional positive regard are two themes that will carry you a long way toward fulfilling this requirement. Regardless of who they are, whose they are, or what they do, students must know there are always caring adults at school supporting their efforts.

Five. Students must be supported by strong and courageous leadership. #1 classrooms must receive support and encouragement on a consistent basis from leaders who understand the difference between management and leadership. For example, these leaders view providing resources to their teachers as a top priority and will preview instruction consistently.

Six. Teachers must offer alternatives. #1 classrooms offer alternatives to any students who meet roadblocks on their path to achieving success. For example, if a student fails a quiz, the #1 classroom provides other opportunities for this student to show mastery. The ultimate goal of this classroom is to have students grasp learning concepts and transfer knowledge.

Seven. Teachers intervene early when there are signs of trouble. #1 classrooms identify trouble early and immediately come up with a plan of action to offset difficulty. For example, if students are struggling with organization, the #1 classroom may assign weekly progress reports for these students as a means of charting progress in all classes.

Eight. Educators must be willing to provide extra time and effort when situations arise. Students benefit greatly from additional assistance from caring adults. It seals the deal in the "capturing" process. When you provide extra time and assistance when needed, it proves to students that you really care about them.

Nine. Educators must involve and respect parents as central partners. During an era when parent involvement is at an all-time low, #1 classrooms must be creative in their approach to involve and respect parents as partners. For example, survey parents and gain their input on meeting times and dates. Also, provide opportunities for parents to gain general knowledge of what their children are learning through their participation in skill sessions, during which teachers provide activities that parents and students can do together to strengthen the skills learned at school.

Ten. Schools must have teachers who teach their students with the same level of quality they want delivered to their own biological children. Failure is never an option for our own children, so we should demand success for the children of others.

Creating Effective Classrooms for All Learners

In order to have a #1 classroom, educators should promote learning with a framework of attitudes and values centered on TRUST. All students should have an opportunity to achieve at a high level and improve in their areas of weakness. Hard work and effective teaching will always be the primary predictors of student achievement in effective classrooms designed for ALL learners to succeed. Students develop trust over time, and once you gain it, you will have numerous opportunities to experience success with your students. They will become active partners in their own learning.

The world is a more interesting place because we are not all the same. As indicated in Chapter 4, there are many different ways to learn and advantages to thinking in different ways. Students who do poorly in school will fare better in #1 classrooms because they become motivated by the simple fact that they will have more success in their learning coupled with the foundation of learning in an environment defined by trust and reciprocal respect.

Here are some pointers for creating a #1 classroom.

Classroom teachers should teach for understanding, not memorization.

Teachers in #1 classrooms organize what they will say to their students in four steps:

1. Purpose
   - Introduction that develops the purpose of the lesson.

2. Active Teaching
   - Remember that the teacher teaches students, not information.

- Avoid rote memorization of information.
- Embed facts and details in the web of understanding.
- Be aware of the power of visuals to organize and clarify information.
- Teach students to use multiple pathways for learning.

3. Summary
   - Begin wrapping up the lesson with a strong conclusion with the assistance of students.

4. Practice
   - Reinforce understanding by applying skills and knowledge to new and related contexts.

Classrooms should provide clear, explicit structures.

- Teachers should give directions both orally and in writing. In addition to oral instructions, directions should always be written on the board for students to see as soon as they enter the classroom.
- Teachers should establish clear routines and daily practices with transitions between activities, and should also involve students in the process of developing routines. The more they are involved in the decisions affecting their learning environment, the better your chances of having them follow the rules.
- Teachers should begin a daily operating system the first day of class and use it consistently throughout the school year. Students are actively involved in the system, and they appreciate consistency. They would rather have bad rules than no rules. Your daily operating system should be a set of practices you and your students follow every day.
- Teachers should use a weekly schedule to provide a concrete overview of what's to come. One way to simplify the review process is to use exercises such as "It's Friday," in which the teacher uses a sponge ball to

highlight three major areas of concentration for the week. The teacher tosses the sponge ball to a student who repeats one of the highlighted areas and passes the ball to another student to do the same. Knowing what is to come helps prepare students to accept responsibility for their learning.

- Visual organizers are often helpful. Some students respond better when they are able to see what they've been a part of and what is ahead for them. Visual organizers continue to be an effective tool to help many students remain engaged.
- Consistency is the key. Students like and need routine and schedules. They like to be able to anticipate what's going to happen and when.

The classroom teacher should teach the skills and information embedded in the curriculum.

- Teach study skills that support success.
- Teach how and when to use memory techniques to master content.
- Model the skills, techniques, and strategies you use as a teacher and learner.
- Recognize language as an essential tool for teaching and learning.
- Assist students with organization: record assignments and due dates, and put dates on handouts.
- Be clear about what students know. Don't make assumptions.

The classroom teacher should intervene early when students are having difficulty learning.

If students don't complete their work, don't assume they don't want to do it. Instead, take steps to explore whether they understand the information and assignments and whether they have the skills to perform the required work.

- Develop techniques to monitor students' understanding as the material is being presented to them.
- Use student errors and difficulties as a tool for planning.

Classrooms should offer alternatives.

- Offer students the gift of time by de-emphasizing its role in the classroom. Students truly appreciate the time given them by a caring teacher or staff member.
- Offer multiple types of assignments and assessments for ALL learners. #1 classrooms provide multiple ways for students to experience success through written and oral assignments or paper-and-pencil tests. Success is the goal.
- Provide multiple opportunities for success. If students in this classroom fall short, give them other opportunities to succeed. The goal is not to give a test grade and move on; it is for students to understand the root meaning of the lessons taught.
- Emphasize understanding and transfer of information. The foundation of a #1 classroom is the development of a value-added relationship between teacher and student where learning is the #1 goal. The ultimate goal is that students grasp concepts and transfer knowledge.

Classrooms should offer unconditional, positive support: regardless of what takes place in the classroom, students know they will always be respected, nurtured, and loved. Today's students need not only a place they feel comfortable and safe in, but also an environment that is not going to change because of an event or action. #1 classrooms provide opportunities for ALL learners to grow educationally, but even more important, to grow as human beings.

CHARACTERISTICS OF #1 CLASSROOM TEACHERS

#1 classroom teachers share the characteristics shown in Figure 6.2 on page 80.

Figure 6.2   Characteristics of a #1 Classroom Teacher

- Is a compulsive listener
- Has a high level of integrity
- Is a great communicator
- Is inquisitive
- Has high expectations for ALL learners
- Is always prepared
- Dresses professionally and appropriately at all times
- Is knowledgeable
- Knows students' names and begins calling them by name the very first day of school
- Resists being sarcastic
- Greets students at the door with a smile each day
- Remembers birthdays and special occasions of students
- Attends events outside of school in which his or her students are participants
- Eats lunch with the students from time to time
- Always expects more of students than the students expect of themselves

Teachers who run #1 classrooms earn respect and admiration from their students by listening to them, motivating them, and delivering quality to them daily.

What other characteristics make #1 teachers?

These classrooms are designed to promote the belief that success is the only option, and teachers who lead this journey truly believe they will encounter these same students in some capacity later in life. For this encounter, they definitely want them to be more than adequately prepared!

A recent conversation with a superintendent reminded me of that fact. He was amazed by the number of his former students who play an active role in his life today. He told me that "never would I imagine that my primary physician would be one of my former students or my electrician or exterminator. They seem to be popping up from everywhere."

I believe that we will see these students again and they will play pivotal roles in our lives.

As we move from being students to being teachers, the other key factor that contributes to success in our #1 classroom is culture, which is described in Figure 6.3.

Figure 6.3   #1 Classroom Culture

1. Praise the good work of your students, and accentuate the positive—students tend to learn better and faster when they feel successful.

2. Become "family" with your students. This is the core of the #1 classroom culture. Students will grow to trust you and depend on this connection to get them through difficult times and experiences.

3. Return assignments or papers to students within a reasonable amount of time.

4. Insist on neatly written work.

5. Insist on work being delivered on time.

6. Call or visit the homes of your students to share positive news.

7. Allow for flexibility in your classroom.

8. Involve students in the planning and delivery of lessons.

9. Become as knowledgeable as possible about the world of your students.

10. NEVER give up on a student.

MANAGING THE CLASSROOM CLIMATE

Classroom behavior continues to rank as one of the major issues we face in educating all learners. The following practical strategies will help teachers ensure that success is the only option for all students.

Which characteristics have you used and how did students in your classroom receive each trait?

When a student

Is talkative, talks out of turn, makes fun of others, or draws attention to himself or herself and surroundings:

- Make eye contact with the student
- Give limited time and attention to behavior
- Give individual attention to the student during breaks
- Ask the student for help during conversation
- Allow the student time to reflect on behavior
- Give the student praise when not behaving in this manner

Is resistant:

- Remain calm and polite
- Remain in control of the classroom, as others are paying attention to how you respond
- Don't disagree, but respond with authority
- Allow him or her a way to gracefully retreat from the confrontation
- Ignore the behavior and focus on other students
- Talk privately with the student as soon as the situation presents itself

Is engaged in a side conversation:

- Ask the talkers if they would like to share their ideas
- Ask their opinions on the topic being discussed
- Stand near the talkers
- Don't embarrass the talkers
- As a last resort, stop talking and wait for them to stop (it won't take long)

For the record, **always allow students to save face.** In a struggle between a teacher and a student, the student will always win. In a #1 classroom, the teacher creates win-win situations with the students. The respect and admiration of the teacher will transfer into students working really hard to accomplish classroom goals and ultimately into their continued success.

Chapter Summary

#1 classrooms promote learning through the development of a foundation of trust between teachers and students. Multiple measures of success lay the groundwork for many students who are not accustomed to achieving academically to finally have a chance. #1 classroom teachers are prepared to find multiple right answers for students and believe that success comes in many forms. This classroom culture is engaging and stimulating for teachers and students and is based on reciprocal respect. Students play a pivotal role in managing this climate as the teacher serves more as a facilitator than as a strong disciplinarian.

Chapter 7 releases the potential of all educators through a three-step process designed to capture the attention of learners, inspire them, and then actively teach them. At the very core of education is the ability we all have to teach. The struggle is to figure out how much our students desire learning. In the next chapter, the reader will gain a better understanding of the power we possess in and out of our classrooms to save our students, one by one.

7

Capture, Inspire, Teach

Three Steps to Effective Teaching and Learning

Understanding ALL learners—their cultures, experiences, values, and beliefs—will enable you to teach them more effectively.

By the end of this chapter, in order to bring your best stuff every day, you should understand the following:

- How to Capture Students
- How to Inspire Students
- How to Teach Students
- How to Celebrate Teaching

Teaching was not the profession I chose. It chose me! I was on my way toward achieving my lifelong dream of becoming a professional basketball player, something I'd prepared for all my life. Suddenly, at the end of my college career, I was not drafted, and I was thrown for the biggest loop I'd ever experienced. However, my sulking did not last very long as I needed every ounce of energy to absorb the experience I was to have with my first class of students.

We all agree that students today are different from those in years past in many respects. Because of this, we need a different approach to educate them. I was well aware of most of these differences, but had very little knowledge of what it would take to reach the students in my class. What I needed was not taught in my undergraduate or graduate school curriculum. I needed a relationship with my students before I set out to teach them.

I will always remember Mrs. Black, one of my former teachers, and I'm sure most of my classmates will too. She was one of those teachers who instantly made you feel like you were hers second only to your home or mother. She went out of her way to greet us at the door each day with a smile on her face. She was dressed up every day, and we noticed. She was well spoken and would share things with us about herself and her family.

Describe a "Mrs. Black" who influenced you as a student. What characteristics did this person possess?

Mrs. Black also came to school every day—literally. She made learning fun and rewarded us all the time for working hard and accomplishing the things that people became amazed we were accomplishing. In other people's eyes, we were not supposed to be achieving and having fun while doing so. In Mrs. Black's eyes, we were. It was as simple as that.

Thinking back, you, too, must have a teacher or teachers you will always remember.

For many of us, these teachers set the standards by which we operate. They taught us much more than our core subjects. They taught us about right and wrong, how to carry ourselves, how to dress professionally, the importance of public speaking, how to develop confidence, and much more. They were our heroes.

As students, we were able to learn in classrooms with these teachers because they created positive relationships with us that they could build on over time. Regardless of where students were from or what color they were, or what socioeconomic status they hailed from, these teachers treated us the same because each child was valued the same. The results teachers recorded were amazing. We students responded positively to them because we felt that these teachers genuinely cared about us. School and education were at the center of our lives.

Unfortunately, that's not always the case today. I recently observed a high school world history class session on the Industrial Revolution. The teacher was trying her best to hold her students' attention. One student slipped his hand into his book bag and pulled out a catalog from Foot Locker, the athletic clothing store. Essentially, he changed channels on his teacher. It was as though he picked up the remote and tuned into something more interesting.

Today's students are a tough audience and differ greatly from those of past decades. They bring to school with them a consumer mentality. If they don't find their teachers interesting, they will decide to tune out. Moreover, they seem to require additional assistance getting engaged in learning, in part because they have become consumers of entertainment and sensationalism; iPods, video games, and cell phones travel with them wherever they go as they look to the world around them to excite and entertain them. Additionally, they search for things to fill the voids created by an emptiness they can't explain. So, when they sit in a classroom, there can be a letdown of sorts because they begin to compare the feeling of excitement and interest they have from outside the classroom to what they're experiencing in the classroom. Sitting in the classroom doesn't stand a chance with today's students compared to playing video games or watching podcasts unless schools and teachers understand and effectively use the three-step process this chapter describes, which will bring our students back from the brink of possible self-destruction.

How to Capture Students

It's commonly known that we cannot teach a student until we have established an appropriate relationship with him or her. Typically, there has to be buy-in on the part of the student. Generally, today's students will only allow you into their world if they feel you have something to offer them. Therefore, the first step in this process is called CAPTURING. Before we can effectively teach today's students, we must first capture their hearts and minds.

Capture means to secure, seize, or take over. It's the first and most critical step in getting students involved in their learning! This process begins the very first day of school and is constantly reinforced through varied experiences throughout the entire year. Teachers who capture their students have standard operating procedures and clear and specific goals, are able to lend an ear, and can discern when students are in need. Their students think there is something special about them, and students work harder for them. They want these teachers to be proud of them. In my case, my teacher, Mrs. Black, thought I was smarter than I was, so I was. She captured me with her expectations, with her belief in me as a student. She saw in me what I didn't see in myself.

It's always amazing to see that diamond in the rough begin to shine. Teachers who can accept students at their current level and then take them to the next one have the ability to capture their students. An accurate measure of whether you are on the right path toward capturing your students is to remind yourself of the teachers who captured you and the special attributes they exhibited in their classes.

What attributes do you like in teachers?

Ways to Capture Your Students

- Attend events they are participating in outside of the classroom, such as sports, community activity, church, Boys and Girls Club, etc.

- When they walk in on the first day of school, have an honor roll banner displayed with their names on it. They should begin the year with all A's in all grade levels.
- Assign students to managerial duties to make them part of your management team. Duties include passing out papers, collecting assignments, assisting with the desks and chairs, and summarizing today's lesson.
- Ask them questions about how they would like their class time to be spent.
- Allow them to make suggestions on how to make classroom culture better.
- Use some of their ideas to ensure that they know you are listening and believe in their ability to make concrete suggestions that may work.
- Exercise flexibility and allow them to make mistakes and learn from them without being cast away.
- Be consistent with rules and policies in all your dealings with ALL students.
- Treat ALL of your students the same because their value is the same.

How to Inspire Students

Inspire means to stimulate, arouse, or motivate. This is the second critical step in getting today's students involved in learning. We cannot expect students to be excited about learning if we are not excited about teaching. Today's students discern your level of excitement not only about what you're teaching, but also about whom you are teaching. It is often necessary to become creative in your approach to make content relevant and exciting to your students. As with the first step in this process, this begins with the very first encounter with your students and is a top priority each day.

Teachers who inspire their students before and while teaching them are, in reality, making deposits. When they encounter difficulty, as we know they will, they can make withdrawals from those deposits.

Ways to Inspire Your Students

- Dress professionally each day.
- Share yourself with your students: the books you read, your dreams, your experiences.
- Involve them in the process of their learning.
- Invite them to be a part of something you're involved in outside of school.
- Teach them to give back.
- Allow them to appreciate seeing you work hard every day.
- Develop powerful connections with ALL students.
- Invite other professionals into your classroom who mirror the dreams and aspirations of your students.
- Expose your students to the world unknown to them.
- Allow each student to experience some form of success each day.

What inspires you to do your best? How can you inspire your students?

How to Teach Students

The final step in the process is to teach students—in other words, to provide knowledge or help. Teaching is a calling, and we are the last hope for the majority of our students. We hold the key that unlocks the door of opportunity for each of them. As our students walk into our classrooms daily, they do so seeking to be understood by adults who spend too much time getting them to understand. The third step in the process is easier than the first two because of our students. Once they are captured and inspired, they will give you their permission to teach them!

Once these three steps become the foundation of the developing culture in your classroom, amazing experiences begin to take shape. Students will have more of a reason for coming to school, so attendance should improve. They will pay closer attention to when assignments are due and will make an effort to complete these assignments and turn them in. This should result in better academic achievement.

Students should have a desire to produce good work daily for the teacher who captures and inspires them. As a result of this three-step process, you will create a classroom where students are truly your partners in teaching and learning. This creates a powerful connection that is focused on success for ALL learners. Each person will fulfill his or her responsibility toward the ultimate goal of believing and achieving.

Ways to Teach Your Students

- Teach with passion.
- Teach with understanding.
- Teach with compassion.
- Teach with power and authority.
- Teach with creativity.
- Teach with knowledge and preparation.
- Teach with all learning styles in mind.
- Teach with input and feedback from your students.
- Teach with multiple goals in mind.
- Teach with flexibility—groups, one-on-one, after school, before school, during lunch.
- Teach within the framework of district-level and school-level goals.
- Teach with one final goal in mind: success for ALL learners.

Many of our former teachers taught with conviction because of what they believed their students were capable of achieving. Deep in their hearts they felt responsible for any student who for whatever reason did not succeed. They took it personally. As we attempt to capture, inspire, and teach a new generation of learners, it is critical that we are honest in our appraisal of our beliefs.

It is also important that we do the following:

- Become conscious of our own beliefs, feelings, and experiences as we engage in delivering quality services to our students.
- Understand the power of our beliefs—what we believe has a profound effect on how we behave and react.

- Understand that belief is confidence in an alleged fact without positive proof.
- Understand that we must rise above societal problems and issues related to those who happen to be different.
- Understand our students and their histories, cultures, and ways of life.

Transferring our beliefs to school and classroom situations can create drama if we're not careful to examine and properly dispose of beliefs that can cause harm to our students, even unintentional harm. These create blind spots that will set you back in the capture, inspire, and teach process. For example, if we are not convinced that all students are capable of learning at a high level, we will transfer that belief in some form to those students affected. As trust is built with students, we must remain sensitive to the fact that they still may not quite believe this is real. They've been let down and put down by so many adults in their lives that many of them constantly wonder "why is this going to last?"

Engagement

The first two steps in the capture, inspire, and teach process open the door to active student engagement. The relationship has been established, creating a foundation you can build on. Even after you experience initial success with hard-to-reach students using this process, there is more work to be done to ensure ongoing success. We must understand the need to bring our best stuff every day. After talking with teachers, it becomes evident that this is easier said than done. How, then, do we increase the chances that we will have more good days than bad? How do we ensure success of some kind for ALL of our students?

- Come to school each day rested from the previous day. It is difficult to use energy for tomorrow today. You will fizzle before the end of the week.

- Come to school healthier each day. Begin a light exercise program if you've not exercised in a while. Begin by stretching, and then walking for 20 minutes three or four times a week.
- Rediscover hobbies you used to enjoy, but somehow got away from. This will create balance and allow you to come to school with a fresh approach each day.
- Collaborate with other teachers working in similar environments. There are many ways to assist or receive assistance from them.
- Develop a good rapport with your administrators. This is your support system.
- Get involved with professional development organizations and attend workshops to keep you up to date on researched-based best practices for working with students and other educators.

The most important thing is that each of us understands our general and specific roles in this mission to recapture the most important profession known to man.

When we teach, we must always do so with our own biological children in mind. We must deliver the same quality to our students each day that we would want a teacher delivering to our own children at home. Our students deserve nothing less.

Additionally, we must remember the following:

- Success for ALL learners is contingent upon our combined efforts to capture, inspire, and teach each student regardless of background, race, or socioeconomic status.
- Success is determined by each student's ability to navigate the system and make adjustments to the school's behavioral norms and the expectations of teachers and other school officials.
- The most powerful tool the school has is each student's need for social connections. Once we get them there, we must capture, inspire, and teach them.

- The majority of students who present problems are those who are experiencing some form of alienation—those who feel unaccepted or rejected for some reason.
- The overall goal of each school must be inclusion versus exclusion.
- Schools must take into account the academic, emotional, social, and psychological development of each student.
- All students are entitled to the education they need at any given time in each developmental stage.

How to Celebrate Teaching

Observing classroom instruction and behavior has always been at the top of my list as a potential means of having an opportunity to "better our best." In my travels, I am often asked to observe teachers doing what they do best, TEACH! Over the years, I have come to rely on essential questions to open up dialogue about the lessons observed instead of just giving feedback on what I observed. This process puts the teachers in charge of their own destiny of bettering their best.

Without a doubt, we have some phenomenal teachers in our schools, teachers who understand their power and authority to restore hope to students who have lost hope. Additionally, we have teachers who appropriately assemble a careful balance of *what* they teach with *how* they teach. They make learning fun for their students and create powerful connections establishing a foundation of success for ALL learners.

What an honor it is for our students to have great teachers who understand that "good" is no longer good enough for our students or schools. Effective schools have, at their very core, the belief in their collective ability to deliver their very best every day. When one falls short, he or she knows there are others teaching beyond their capacity on any given day. These teachers have saved the lives of countless students who otherwise would be lost to the street, crime, prisons, or death. **We celebrate each of you as you continue to capture, inspire, and teach.**

CHAPTER SUMMARY

It has become increasingly difficult to engage today's students in the teaching and learning process without forming a relationship founded on mutual respect. When teachers capture and inspire their students, it opens the door for teaching and learning to occur. Moreover, it lays the foundation for teachers and students to discover the mastery of education together.

Chapter 8 closes the book with specific A-to-Z tips for survival. It guides teachers to the place we all desire: a safe and secure environment for all students where all are respected, encouraged, and taught by the very best this world has to offer.

8

Survival Tips for Today's Teachers and Leaders

There is a new requirement to qualify to teach or lead in a school district today. It is to survive while holding on to our passion for educating ALL learners.

Ty the end of this chapter, in order to bring your best stuff every day, you should understand the following:

- How to Set the Tone for Survival
- How to Be a Successful Teacher
- The ABCs of Survival
- Hope

There are those who have come into our profession burning with passion, but leave overcome with pain—the pain of knowing they had the knowledge to give, but could not find ways to transfer what they knew to the reluctant learners we face today. Then, there are those who enter our profession lacking some of the prerequisite knowledge, but are gifted in their ability to develop powerful connections with their students to the degree that they actually begin learning together. These "connections" serve as a lifeline that helps teachers and leaders accomplish much more than simply surviving.

HOW TO SET THE TONE FOR SURVIVAL

From my discussions with former teachers and administrators, I learned that there have been common elements used in efforts to capture, inspire, and teach ALL learners. If it worked for us, it may work for you. Some of the beliefs we shared and used in our work with students hailing from all backgrounds and cultures are listed below. We hope this helps.

Figure 8.1   Tips for Capturing, Inspiring, and Teaching Students

- Realize that the first few days of meeting and interacting with your students is a time to capture and inspire your students, not have them turn to page 10 in their textbook. Get to know their names and find out what is important to them.
- If you are fairly new to teaching, realize that you will probably learn more in your first few years in the classroom than you did all four years of college.
- Don't be afraid to ask the more experienced teachers for assistance or guidance. While doing so, make sure you are seeking advice from the right ones, as this could backfire on you if you approach veteran teachers whose fire is no longer lit. They will offer you no more than additional issues and stress.
- Visit other classrooms to get an idea of theme creation for your school. You can gather ideas that may complement those of others on your team.
- Find a mentor in your school to work with you and use this person's expertise. This will prove to be invaluable as you develop your own teaching style and belief system.

- Be prepared to deal with issues you may not have received training on, as many students will bring into your classroom situations you are not accustomed to dealing with.
- Develop a support system that is inclusive of other teachers who are experiencing some of the same things you are experiencing. It's always good to know you are not alone.
- Learn to accept constructive criticism from those qualified to give it. It could prove to be invaluable.
- Learn to laugh at yourself when you make mistakes. Trust me, this will not be your last.
- Develop quality lesson plans that promote active learning and keep your students engaged.
- Remember, teaching is a career, not a job!

HOW TO BE A SUCCESSFUL TEACHER

Success is determined by the accomplishment of goals. A successful teacher achieves the task of effectively teaching ALL students. But, simply teaching our students today is not enough. Good teachers are leaving our profession each year at a rapid pace, realizing that good is no longer good enough. It simply does not cut it anymore. We seek great teachers who go beyond teaching subject areas to capture, inspire, and enrich students' minds and spirits. Great teachers will always prevail.

The integrity and honor of our profession rest with each and every one of you who will not only stick it out to the end, but will do so with such style and grace that we will know victory in the end for each of our students. We will attract quality teachers who understand that when there is a "call," we must find multiple right answers to break the pattern of mediocrity and waste. We must find in ALL of our students the place of most potential, develop it, and set them on their way to realize their biggest dreams. We must see the extraordinary through ordinary eyes.

THE ABCs OF SURVIVAL

Accept your calling.

Bring your best stuff every day.

Communicate with your students, administrators, parents, staff, and other teachers.

Develop stamina for long, action-packed days.

Empower your students.

Failure should be removed from your vocabulary.

Get to know as many students and staff members as possible at your school.

Have high expectations for ALL students.

Implement clear, consistent policies and procedures.

Justify what you are doing.

Keep an even temperament.

Learn as much as you can as often as you can.

Model desired attitudes and behaviors for your students.

Never let them see you sweat.

Over-plan, as having too much is always better than not having enough.

Prepare exciting lessons.

Quit worrying about what others are doing and pave your way to success.

Reward good classroom behavior and success.

Stay away from gossipers and negative attitudes

Take risks.

Understand that you may be the last hope for many of your students.

Volunteer to share with others the ideas and experiences that are working for you.

Work hard every day, ALL day.

Xpect the unexpected and plan for it.

Yell for help when you need it.

Zero in on your strengths and be determined to survive!

HOPE

Education continues to be the wisest choice of many alternatives offered to us in the free world. It is the vehicle that directly links us to opportunities otherwise not afforded us.

As we embrace our call, we must see the light that shines off the faces of our students who finally made it through the struggles, the ups and downs. We never gave up on them, so they never gave up on themselves. We are the chosen few who will always give that which has been placed in us to give: guidance, encouragement, love, direction, and HOPE.

Although we suffer tremendous losses daily among our students, we also experience success as many of our students come through for us, for their families and communities, and for themselves. Schools have been around for centuries and will be around for many to come. Let us maintain our commitment to make our schools learning communities that create hope and produce success for every student every day. **Our mission is to leave no student out!**

SUMMARY

Highly effective schools have found a way to establish an effective culture. The foundation of this culture is established by a commitment by all to ensure success for every student.

At the heart of this book are the need to understand today's student, our ability to connect with them, and a collaborative approach to educate them.

In years past, students entered our schools and classrooms socially adept and ready to learn from teachers they respected because they were taught to respect them. Home was the number one influence on students during this era; it served as a support system to the school and teachers. It was a win-win situation for all involved in the most important journey we could take.

Many of today's schools are struggling because each year heavier and heavier demands are placed on them. Students are no longer coming to school prepared to learn, nor are they socially prepared to accept the responsibility to rise to the expectations set forth by schools that are trying to turn things around.

Courageous leadership, well-prepared teachers, and support staff working synergistically will produce better results when they adapt to the needs of the ever-changing student who enters our doors on a daily basis. This book examines the expanded role of school leader, teacher, and supporting casts, as well as the reasons many of our students do not perform well in our schools.

During this period of standardized test accountability and anxiety, this book offers the reader opportunities to better understand their options as they create meaningful connections and relationships with each student, thus resulting in better outcomes.

From vision to reality, when students are captured and inspired, we increase our chances of receiving their permission to teach them. Several chapters provide classroom strategies that will enable you to release yourself from classroom management duty and unleash the spirit of academic excellence housed in each of your students.

I wrote *Teaching to Capture and Inspire All Learners* to provide practical strategies for school leaders and teachers to be able to adopt and begin implementing immediately. Now, at your fingertips, you have specific tips that can help turn your vision into operational strategies.

References

Beane, J. A. (1997). *Curriculum integration: Designing the core of democratic education*. New York: Teachers College Press.

Buzan, T. (1976). *Use both sides of your brain*. New York: Dutton.

Black, S. (1994). Different kinds of smart. *The Executive Educator, 16*(1), 24–27.

Bruning, R. H., Schraw, G. J., & Ronning, R. R. (1999). *Cognitive psychology and instruction* (3rd ed.). Upper Saddle River, NJ: Prentice Hall.

Cawelti, G. (1995). *Handbook of research on improving student achievement*. Arlington, VA: Educational Research Service.

The Center for Reclaiming America. (1997). *Issues Tearing Our Nation's Fabric: Breakdown of the Family*. Retrieved July 18, 2007, from http://www.leaderu.com/issues/fabric/chap03.html

Davison, K., Francis, L., & Birch, L. (2005). Links between parents' and girls' television viewing behaviors: A longitudinal examination. *The Journal of Pediatrics, 147*(4), 436–442.

Dolan, W. P. (1993). World-class schools: A time for change. In *Advancing the national education goals: The role of collective bargaining*. Washington, DC: National Education Association.

Dunn, K., & Dunn, R. (1987). Dispelling outmoded beliefs about student learning. *Educational Leadership, 44*(6), 55–62.

Dunn, R., & Dunn, K. (1978). *Teaching students through their individual learning styles: A practical approach*. Reston, VA: Prentice Hall.

Elmore, R. (2000). *Building a new structure for school leadership*. Washington, D.C.: Albert Shanker Institute.

Epstein, J. L., & Mac Iver, D. J. (1992). *Opportunities to learn: Effects on eighth graders of curriculum offerings and instructional approaches* (Report #34). Baltimore: Center for Research on Effective Schooling for Disadvantaged Students. Office of Educational Research and Improvement, Washington, D.C.

Farkas, S., Johnson, J., Duffet, A., & Foleno, T. (2001). *Trying to stay ahead of the game: Superintendents and principals talk about school leadership*. New York: Public Agenda.

Gardner, H. (1983). *Frames of mind: The theory of multiple intelligences.* New York: Basic Books.

Gay, G. (2000). *Culturally responsive teaching: Theory, research, and practice.* New York: Teachers College Press.

Gerloff, P. (1998). The power of self-connections: Transforming adults to reclaim the children. In J. T. Gibson (Ed.), *Educating the throw-away children: What we can do to help students at risk.* New directions for school leadership #6. San Francisco: Jossey-Bass.

Grissmer, D., & Kirby, S. H. (1997). Teacher turnover and teacher quality. *Teachers College Record, 99*(1), 45–56.

Ingersoll, R. (2001). Teacher turnover and teacher shortages: An organizational analysis. *American Educational Research Journal, 38*(3), 499–534.

Ingersoll, R., & Smith, T. (2003). The wrong solution to the teacher shortage. *Educational Leadership, 60*(8), 30–33.

Jackson, P. W. (1986). *The practice of teaching.* New York: Teachers College Press.

Leon, S., & Elias, M. (1998). A comparison of portfolio, performance and traditional assessment in the middle school. *Research in Middle Level Educational Quarterly, 21*(92), 21–37.

Literary reading in dramatic decline, according to National Endowment for the Arts Survey. (2004, July 8). Retrieved August 17, 2007 from http://www.nea.gov/news/news04/readingatrisk.html

Liu, E., Kardos, S. M., Kauffman, D., Peske, H. G., & Johnson, S. M. (2000). Barely breaking even: Incentives, rewards, and the high costs of choosing to teach. Retrieved August 13, 2007 from http://www.gse.harvard.edu

Louis, K. S., & Kruse, S. (1995). *Professionalism and community: Perspectives on reforming urban schools.* Thousand Oaks: Corwin Press.

Mazzeo, C. (2003). Improving teaching and learning by improving school leadership. Issue Brief, September 12, 2003. Washington, DC: National Governors Association Center for Best Practices.

Montuori, D. (2003). Urban youth: An elusive, but lucrative, population to target for consumer goods marketers. *Packaged Facts.* Retrieved August 13, 2007 from http://www.packagedfacts.com/editor/viewcontent.asp?prid=244

Nash, R. (n.d.). *America's public schools: Crisis and cure.* Grand Rapids, MI: Acton Institute for the Study of Religion and Liberty. Retrieved August 17, 2007 from http://www.acton.org/ppolicy/education/ppolicy_education_school_crisis_crisis.php

Newmann, F. (2001). Instructional program coherence: What is it and why it should guide school improvement. *Educational Evaluation and Policy Analysis, 23*(4), 297–304.

Oxley, D. (1994). Organizing schools into small units: Alternatives to homogeneous grouping. *Phi Delta Kappan, 75*, 521–526.

Peters, S. (2001). *Inspired to learn: Why we must give children hope.* Marietta, GA: Rising Sun Publishing.

Peters, S. G. (2006). *Do you know enough about me to teach me?* (2nd ed., expanded version). Orangeburg, SC: The Peters Group Foundation.

Portin, B., Schneider, P., DeArmond, M., & Gundlach, L. (2003). *Making sense of leading schools: A study of the school principalship.* Seattle: Center for Reinventing Public Education, Daniel J. Evans School of Public Affairs, University of Washington.

Powell, A. (2007). *Hip hop hypocrisy: When lies sound like the truth.* Lincoln, NE: iUniverse.

Rosenshine, B. (1971). *Teaching behaviours and student achievement.* London: National Foundation for Educational Research in England and Wales.

Russell, J. F. (1997). Relationships between the implementation of middle-level program concepts and student achievement. *Journal of Curriculum and Supervision, 12*, 152–168.

Schiff, T. (2002). Principals' readiness for reform: A comprehensive approach. Retrieved August 13, 2007 from http://mff.org/newsroom/news.taf?page=312

Sebring, P., & Bryk, A. (2000). School leadership and the bottom line in Chicago. *Phi Delta Kappan, 81*(6), 440–443.

Shumow, L., & Harris, W. (1998, April). *Teachers' thinking about home-school relations in low-income urban communities.* Paper presented at the annual meeting of the American Educational Research Association, San Diego, CA.

Stiggins, R. (2002). Assessment for learning. *Education Week, 21*(26), 30–33.

Tomlinson, C. A. (1999). *The differentiated classroom: Responding the needs of all learners.* Alexandria, VA: ASCD.

Thornburgh, N. (2006, April 9). Dropout nation. *Time* [Electronic version]. Retrieved July 18, 2007 from http://www.time.com/time/magazine/article/0,9171,1181646,00.html

Villegas, A. M., & Lucas, T. (2002). Preparing culturally responsive teachers. *Journal of Teacher Education, 53*(1), 20-32.

White, J. (2003). *Teamwork and empowerment.* Columbus, OH: Performance Consulting, Inc.

Wiggins, G., & McTighe, J. (1998). *Understanding by design.* Alexandria, VA: ASCD.

Index